BOYCRAZY:

And how I ended up Single & (mostly) Sane

by Tiffany Dawn

ISBN: 150089270X
ISBN-13: 978-1500892708

Some names have been changed
to protect the privacy of certain individuals.

Edited by Kelly Hopson
Cover design by Kirsten Reilly

Unless otherwise stated, all Bible references
are taken from the NKJV:
Hayford, J. W. (Gen. Ed.). (1979, 1982, 1991)
Spirit Filled Life Bible: New King James Version
Nashville: Thomas Nelson Publishers

To my littlest sister, Amy,
who is already wiser than I am
when it comes to boys.

ACKNOWLEDGMENTS

In just a couple weeks I'll hold this finished book in my hands. (Let me take a moment to shout for joy!) Writing Boycrazy has stretched me beyond my comfort zone — in a good way. I wanted it to be perfect, to say everything that possibly needed to be said on this subject, but one book can't do that. In the end, after wrestling through my own, intimidating self-expectations, I've simply written my story.

Thank you to the incredible focus groups who read this book before its release and gave valuable feedback: Adrienne Meyer, Amy Robison, Deb Cline, Grace Oliver, Hannah Decker, Janae Stacy, Julia Robison, Karyn Raney, Michelle Cronk, Rebekah Hazleton, and Traci Morley. Your insights made all the difference! James Dick, thank you for patiently reading every single chapter out loud to me so I could hear it for myself, and giving honest and insightful feedback.

To the women who invested their time and talent to make this book look and sound fabulous: Kirsten Reilly (cover design) and Kelly Hopson (editing) — THANK YOU!! To Traci Morley for pouring over this manuscript with me for hours, helping design the interior and making it look super fun — you are wonderful!

To the dear friends and mentors who have taught me so much about relationships, singleness, and becoming the person God made me to be: the Cronks, the DuPrés, James, Joanna, Joel, Justin, Karyn, Kellie, Krysta, Rick, and Track. Thank you for sharing this journey with me in honest love, and standing by me when I was…well, let's just say I was a wee bit obsessed with good-looking men.

Thank you to my family: To my mom, for challenging and encouraging me to write this story, even when I didn't know if I could. To my dad, for believing that I can do anything, and helping me reach my dreams in practical ways. To my siblings: Liyah, Andrew, Isaac, and Amy, for your humor that zests our life, for truly loving me even when I was (really) annoying, and for your honesty.

Jesus. I have to pause here because where do I even begin? Thank you Lord for everything. For your mercy that rescues me, your grace that carries me, your love that surrounds me. Thank you for recycling every ounce of brokenness in my life so that it can help someone else. Thank you for the opportunity to share this story, and helping me write it down even when I felt overwhelmed, not knowing what to say. Would you be glorified in these pages? Would you reach out and touch hearts? Let this be a moment when the Divine intersects with our fragile humanity.

TABLE OF CONTENTS

4: THE SEMESTER ABROAD 66

I spent my final semester of college studying abroad in the enchanted land of Australia. While there, I realized the hypocritical ways I approached guy relationships.

5: THE DREAMING YEARS 89

After graduating college, although I felt suffocated by singleness, I also began to find joy and purpose as dreams inside me came to life.

6: THE TRAVIS YEARS 110

Another man came into my life around my 24th birthday, as I began to wonder what it meant to fall in love, and how to know if someone was "the one."

7: SINGLE AND SANE 155

Suddenly everything changed when God began to make all things new in my life.

IF YOU'RE CURIOUS 182

This section is for all of you who (like me) crave closure. It tells the end of the story with each of the guys I dated and a new story that has only just begun...

DEAR READER

My name is Tiffany Dawn, and I'm a 27-year-old girl who's fallen in love many, many times. *And I'm not just talking about boys.* I've fallen for weird fashion trends, ice cream, summer, the color coral, gluten-free pretzels (try them, seriously), shopping, sparkles, writing, historical fiction, traveling, and most recently, everything spy-related. I just love it all! But long before I ever fell in love with spies, or really anything else on that list, I tripped head over heels over the idea of marriage. My goal since childhood? To find my Prince Charming and get some major bling on my left ring finger ASAP, thank you very much!

You see, as a little girl running wild in 18th century hoop skirts (yes, I may have been born in the wrong century), I held two dreams for my life: I wanted to be a missionary and I wanted to get married. All this would happen preferably in the following order: Get married by age 20, move with my husband to China by age 21, and there be martyred together. (*I know, I know.* What 7-year-old dreams of being killed because of her faith?)

The missions dream evolved over the years into something of a speaker and author, rather than a martyr, so now I travel around the country for several months a year speaking on girls' issues — more particularly, on the topic of my first book: <u>The Insatiable Quest for Beauty</u>.[1] (Best. Job. Ever.) My mom is very thankful for that development, particularly the part in which I'm still alive.

---

[1] *My first book, <u>The Insatiable Quest for Beauty</u>, shares my journey through disordered eating, poor body image, and an obsession with perfection.*

The marriage goal, however, is still crouching in the back of my mind as I sit here, a few weeks before my 28th birthday. (Feel free to send gluten-free pretzels in the mail with a birthday card!) Funny how time flies, and still...*no ring on my finger*. Oddly enough, I'm finally okay with that. I feel like I've reached a point in my life that I never thought existed: a place where I'm single *but also* mostly sane. (I was going to say single *and* sane, but my family informed me that I am not, and never will be, completely sane.) Finding sanity in my singleness hasn't been easy, especially when this dream of marriage has come up to taunt me more times than I care to remember.

The most recent time was last summer, a year ago now, although I can conjure it up in my mind like it was just yesterday. Actually, I may even have been working on this book the day he called me up — the man I thought I loved — with a sense of urgency in his voice:

"What are you doing right now?" he asked. "I'm right by your house. Can we meet up to talk?"

What was I doing? Well, I'll tell you what I *hadn't* done. I hadn't showered. No makeup. No cute clothes. Not exactly the "let's talk" look I'd usually go for. But I had waited ten years for this talk, and if he was ready, well I was more than ready.

We met at the Starbucks near my parents' house to grab coffee, but he couldn't sit still. "Let's take a walk," he said, so I led the way across the plaza's parking lot, toward a side path weaving along a stream. Before we reached the path, he'd already blurted out, "Okay, if we have this conversation, it won't hurt our friendship, right? Because I don't want to lose you. I don't want this to change everything if it doesn't work out."

"I promise." Tugging a corner of my mouth into a grin, I thought of all we'd been through together. Then of all we *hadn't* experienced together. "However, if one of us marries someone else, it will change everything," I added. "Eventually, our relationship will be different than it is now. It's about time we stop being afraid of that."

"That's true. I just don't want it to change yet." He drew his hand over his face and took a deep breath. "Tiff, the truth is: I have feelings for you, and I have since the day I met you, when you were 17-years-old."

I barely looked up from the path we had reached and could scarcely breathe for fear of breaking the moment's spell. My voice slid out in a whisper, "I feel the same way."

Little did I know, standing in that moment, that things are not always as they seem.

This book you hold in your hands is my story of growing up as a boy-crazy girl, always dreaming of marriage and waiting for life to start once my prince charming had arrived. It's also a collection of heartaches, fears, and (just for fun) some weird date stories. This book isn't meant as theology, but as an encouragement to ask the hard questions about dating.

While writing this manuscript, I've been praying, "Lord, would you please touch lives through this book? Would you let this actually make a difference for people?"

And here's the beautiful thing: All this book contains are the lessons I've learned; carefully woven into the narrative of my life story. That seems so little to offer, and yet if Jesus fed five thousand people with only five loaves of bread and two fish, I have to wonder if there is anything too small to offer Him. When His greatness intersects with our smallness, it feeds the hungry, heals the broken, and brings life to those who have died inside.

I pray that this book is like those five loaves and two fish. I pray that the Holy Spirit would breathe life inside of you as you read my story and that this book would be a conduit for His work. Whatever your background, whatever your journey, I hope you'll find that some of the things I've learned, speak to you as well.

As you're reading, check out:

www.tiffanydawn.net/boycrazy

for further resources to go with each chapter. I'm praying for you, and I hope I get to hear a piece of *your* story someday!

With love,

Tiffany Dawn

1 THE ERIC YEARS

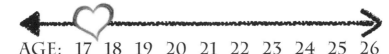

AGE: 17 18 19 20 21 22 23 24 25 26

Love came into my life with pomp and circumstance, exactly the way I imagined it would: The swirling snow during our first deep hug, the delicious darkness as we stood stargazing into each other's faces, the roses and scrawling notes left on my windshield. If I close my eyes tight enough, I can still see the warm candlelight, hear the soft, groveling jazz, and feel his hand on the small of my back, twirling me around the living room.

It was pure romance — everything my 17-year-old heart desired; the moments I'd spent my life dreaming about. It was a storybook kind of love.

I was wrapped up, head over heels, with this beautiful, talented man. I always knew it would be this way. I always knew we'd meet and in one magical moment, I would know it was *him*. Eric. Man of my dreams.

What they don't tell you in fairytales is how dangerous and cruel love can be. What they don't tell you is that when you're blindly wrapped up in love, sometimes you'd do anything for that person, even if that means remaking yourself, reshaping your values, and recycling your heart. They don't tell you how much power that person has over you; how much pain comes from one *off* glance, one burning word. None of the fairytales show how devastating this beautiful desire can be.

But here I go getting ahead of myself. The only way I can do my story justice is to go back to the very beginning.

— cinderella daydreams —

Since I was a little girl, I've dreamed of the day I would meet *him*. I would be wearing an exquisite dress, suffocating in sparkles and diamonds, with puffed sleeves so gigantic I could hardly fit through the doorway. One day I would be standing on the balcony (I was obsessed with balconies and turrets) overlooking my rose garden and stone walkway... when suddenly, *he* would appear: midnight hair, milk chocolate eyes, and the knowing look of a man smitten by love. He'd slide his arm around my waist and whisk me away to our new home (which, of course, looked just like the Swiss Family Robinson's treehouse, except with chandeliers).

I felt like Cinderella, daydreaming her days away as she swept the floor and cleaned the bathroom, finished her homework and read her Bible, all the while dreaming, dreaming, dreaming of her ever after love.

My parents wisely decreed that this boy-crazy daughter of theirs could not date before age 16. It was kind of nice because then, when no guys were interested, I didn't have to feel bad about myself. I wasn't dating because my parents wouldn't let me. It was because I was too young, not because I wasn't good enough. But in my dreams, I was dancing under the stars with boys with milk chocolate eyes.

— buttercup proms —

I met the man of my dreams at my home school "prom" when I was 15-years-old. It wasn't a balcony, but I was wearing a beautiful dress the color of buttercups, with baby's breath hiding in my long, honey curls. (I'd even tried to match my braces to the color of my prom dress, though it hadn't quite worked out right.)

Shy in the new situation, I was standing on the edge of the dance floor with my friend Katie when this sinfully gorgeous guy walked over. He paused in front of us, and I looked up, not daring to breathe.

For one split moment my heart sputtered. One brief second of hope, not daring to believe it...was he about to invite me onto the dance floor?

The moment burst as his eyes turned to Katie, and he asked her to dance.

That's okay, I comforted myself, *he's way too cute for me anyway. Plus, I can't dance! I wouldn't know what to do with myself.*

I was surprised when Katie said he should dance with me. To be honest, I don't think Eric really wanted to, but he chivalrously led me onto the gleaming dance floor anyway.

There I was in the center of spinning couples, in the moment I'd always dreamed of — when the whole world is supposed to fade away...*and I spent the whole dance staring at my feet.* I was so nervous from having this adorable guy holding me, and afraid I was going to step on his toes, that I never looked up once. Oh, and I danced with him at arms' length. (*Literally,* a full arm's length.)

We didn't dance again that night, nor did I catch his name, but I held the memory in my mind and savored it during my Cinderella daydreams.

— it all begins —

Which brings me up to where I began my story: two years after prom, just after my 17th birthday, when love came into my life with pomp and circumstance, turning the mundane moments of life into something extraordinary.

Lockers slammed shut, voices bounced around every corner as I walked in circles. "Where's music theory?" I finally asked the person I nearly ran over.

"Oh I'm in that class too! First year?" the guy asked, and I nodded. "I think it's over here. Name's Jim."

A small crowd was gathering outside the recital hall, and we found seats at the back. More and more students streamed in, sitting on the floor after the chairs filled.

"Welcome to the music program!" the department head announced, as everyone stilled. "I want you to look around at all the people you've come in with."

College! Well, community college, but still a magical place. I had been homeschooled my entire life, and was about to burst with excitement! How many days had I longed to be surrounded by friends all day long...and by cute guys! Speaking of which, Jim wasn't half bad.

I know, I know, God, I thought. For some bizarre reason I really felt like I wasn't supposed to date this first year of college. *Which I totally didn't agree with.* When other people decided to take a year off of dating, I always thought it was weird and meaningless. Especially because I'd never dated! So what was the point? My whole life had already been focused on God...well, other than my daydreams. *Whatever.* God always won out in our disagreements. And to be honest, if ever I'd known something to be true, it was that I had to be single that year. It was so clear. I couldn't understand why, but I *knew*.

The department head was still speaking. "Take a good look at these people around you. There are 200 of you now, but by the end of this first semester, that will cut in half. Half of you will quit because this program is too rigorous or you can't keep your grades up. By the time you graduate, there'll be only about 25 of you who have graduated in just two years."

My spine straightened as the voice went on, introducing faculty and sharing expectations. All I could think was: *I will be one of those 25.* I had to be. And by then I'd be engaged. After all, I was 17 now. That gave me a year to find a guy, a year to date, and a year to get married by the age of 20. Then I'd graduate with my associate's degree in piano performance so I could teach piano lessons for some extra income while being a stay-at-home wife/missionary, preferably in China. Maybe I'd even meet my future husband during this year off of dating! Wouldn't that be a great story?

"Some welcome speech," Jim grinned as we filed out of the room an hour later. I grinned back. You never knew, maybe Jim was *the one*!

— him —

My friend led the Christian group on campus and invited me to join their weekly meetings. I, in turn, invited Jim and this other guy Matt, who I'd met in the library. (Matt's blue eyes popping against his matching Abercrombie muscle tee made my head spin, so I had immediately locked onto his perfect smile and invited him to join me for the Christian group.)

I was wearing a homemade shirt (and not in a cool way) when I showed up at the first meeting. No one saw me standing in the doorway, so I just searched around the room for an open seat. *Then I froze.* My eyes passed someone familiar and then darted back. Leaning back in a chair, laughing with the girl beside him, sat that guy I'd danced with at prom, while wearing my dress the color of buttercups!

No way. No, no, no way! Is it really...? I slid into a chair just down the row from him. He was bent towards the cute girl, arm draped over her chair. For some strange reason, it hurt me to see him that way. When introductions began, he said his name was Eric. He still hadn't noticed me, *big surprise*. He didn't notice me until I made some apparently intelligent comment halfway through the discussion. Everyone got really quiet, and he looked straight at me. All the shadowy memories clicked into focus. Yes, even though two years ago I had spent the entire dance staring at my feet, I was sure. *It was him!* The guy from the prom; the guy from my dreams.

— Sunflower —

I loved that first semester of college. Constantly surrounded by my new friends, feeling part of something bigger than myself — it was a wonderful life. My friend who led the Christian group on campus asked me to run for president the following semester. (Can you guess my answer? Um, yes!)

On top of my social and spiritual life, a sweet, sweet friendship was growing between Eric and me. He didn't notice me the way I wanted him to, but slowly he appreciated who I was as a person. How I longed for him to think I was beautiful too, in the painfully obvious way he noticed other girls! But for now, if friendship was the only way I could have him in my life, I'd take what I could get.

He started inviting me to his concerts and bringing me back souvenirs from their times on the road. Sometimes it felt like we were on the verge of dating during our late night, three-hour phone calls; during morning prayer meetings, lunches in the cafeteria, and music sessions in the practice rooms; during adventures to each other's churches and family dinners. I felt like his *"special friend"*…but still just a friend. That became clear whenever he'd mention another girl, or start flirting with some other super skinny, pretty chick. When he was done talking with her, he'd come back over to give me a ride home. See? Just friends.

Whatever our relationship status, by the end of that first semester, I couldn't imagine life without Eric. My face was like a sunflower turned toward the sun, drinking in his scent, his voice, his eyes. I wanted to be with him forever.

— clarity —

Over Christmas break during freshman year of college, I took a train into the heart of cornfields and small town America: Fort Wayne, Indiana. Staying with relatives, I spent the month of January away from Eric, seeking time and space to pray.

The memory of God's challenge to be single that year nagged my mind, but I attempted to push it aside and reason it away. Surely I had misheard; Eric was an incredible guy who loved God, led worship, and served in youth ministry (aka, perfect husband material). To top it all off, *I loved him.* I'd already been single my whole life, so what difference would another year make? It wasn't like God to hold out on me...*or was it?*

On the few occasions Eric and I talked long-distance that January, I bounced back and forth across the room with giddy delight, clasping the phone to my ear. Yet each moment spent with God, I wrestled with the elephant in the room.

One night Song of Solomon 4:6 jumped off the pages of my Bible, as though it suddenly morphed into bold font:

"Until the day breaks and the shadows flee away,
I will go my way to the mountain of myrrh
and to the hill of frankincense."

As I read this verse, an image came to me. From my overhead view, I saw myself dancing with arms outstretched on a hill surrounded by mountains. As the image came closer, the only way I could describe it was like the opening scene in "Sound of Music."[2] The sun had not yet peered over the mountains, but a tender lightness in the air gave away its coming prelude. When the image slid to the right, I saw three crosses standing on the hill. Once again I saw myself, now kneeling before the center cross. No one was around. I was alone, but I wasn't afraid. Nor was I sad; it was a beautiful, full solitude.

Right away I recognized the meaning carried within the image. I was standing on the mountain of myrrh and frankincense: two of the spices with which Jesus was prepared for burial. Just as He had died, so I was called to die to this beautiful desire — to surrender my timeline for marriage and relinquish my obsession with finding a boyfriend. Why? *So that in Him I could live.* The full aloneness

---

[2] The Sound of Music, *directed by Robert Wise (UK: Rodgers and Hammerstein), 1965.*

spoke of a sweet, sweet intimacy that I would share with my heavenly Father until the dawn broke into my life, driving away the shadows. Somehow I sensed that when the shadows fled from morning's light, I would see him — the man I prayed for — standing in the rich valley.

A few nights later, I had a beautiful dream: I was reading the Psalms when God began speaking the most incredible, rich words over me. When I awoke, all I remembered was this sentence: "I will be with you always, standing shoulder to shoulder."

It was so clear. I knew what I had to do.

— resolve —

My month away quickly drew to a close. I took the train back to New York, and when it chugged into the station, a portion of my heart fell apart. Dad stood waiting to pick me up where Eric had stood to drop me off only weeks ago: the beginning of the end.

Deflated but peaceful, I leaned against the kitchen counter talking with my family when the doorbell rang. Dad went to answer it, and immediately I heard Eric's voice in snatches of conversation.

"Eric, I thought you forgot about us! We haven't seen you since Tiffany left, why didn't you come visit?" Dad was teasing.

I ran down the hall and flung myself into Eric's arms. All resolve melted away in his warmth. Excuses emerged for every conviction. He was everything I'd ever wanted, everything on my three-page wish list for my future husband. And to top it all off, *I loved him*. What else mattered? *Surely God would understand.*

— something's not right —

"It's like a beach ball that keeps popping to the surface," Eric explained a few days later. I paced my room, scarcely believing my ears. *Was he seriously about to ask me out? And what was this about a beach ball?*

"I wasn't going to court you," Eric continued, "but I can't ignore it. God keeps bringing it back to my attention. I think we're supposed to be together."

I paused in my tracks. Something didn't feel quite right. *What about the kind of man who would pursue me and love me before I ever noticed his existence? Why did it have to be this insistent beach ball convincing him? Did he not love me like I loved him?*

And yet, he was everything I'd ever wanted. My heart beat faster at the thought of his voice, his face.

My parents gave their permission. What an incredible and exciting new chapter of life! I pushed down memories of what God had impressed on my heart amidst the cornfields and basked in the glory of being Eric's girlfriend. After all, courting was different than dating. God probably just wanted me to think about marriage with this guy, rather than waste time dating him.

— the spell —

My world snapped from black and white to high-definition color overnight. Every moment became attuned to Eric's presence or absence. Every nerve stood on end like a magnetic pull within myself. I felt like I couldn't rest without him near me.

I had never known this incredible capacity God gave us! The capacity to fall in love and experience romance; to share our world with a person we couldn't imagine life without.

It was just like God, too. As I looked around, I knew He could have created the world in simple black and white. We wouldn't have known any differently. But instead He mixed a palette of rainbows, giving single colors a myriad of shades.

In the same way, He could have created humans to be solitary creatures, perfectly independent, content to be alone. Instead, He fashioned a desire within our souls to share life with a best friend and lover.

For the first time, I noticed the colors on the trees in autumn, the glorious, silent waltz of a sunset or the symphony of a sunrise. I smelled joy in the crisp Thanksgiving air and wanted to spin with my arms out and eyes closed in the first snowfall. Every time his hand touched my hair or his eyes lingered on mine, every time we were in a room together and it seemed no one was there but the two of us, I was intoxicated; head over heels in love. I fell so hard and so fast I hardly knew how it happened.

— Submission —

It steals your soul away. Love, that is. It invades your thoughts and filters through your mind like sunlight through tree branches, filling up all the empty spaces with its light. It makes you feel like you're floating on bubbles, forgetting how easily those bubbles are broken, how easily you can fall back into gravity's pull.

I would be putting it lightly to say Eric wasn't who I thought he was. I'd spent so much time dreaming about him that I thought he was the perfect guy I'd always imagined. Reality set in quickly. No one is perfect, but I refused to admit it. When pastors and mentors encouraged me to break it off with Eric, I wouldn't listen. I was changing as a person, and not in a good way. My mentors noticed this long before I did, as they

> I'd spent so much time dreaming about him that I thought he was the perfect guy I'd imagined.

observed the way I distanced myself from close friends, and how I began to approach God out of fear instead of love. I'd changed significant pieces of my personality. Instead of listening to their advice as I had in the past, I distanced myself from them. It was easy to blind myself to the truth and only see what I wanted to see, but my feelings weren't so easy to control. One minute I'd be soaring along on his love, and the next I'd want to sink into the ground; grief and betrayal washing over me.

One day I returned from a successful shopping expedition. Eric was kind of old-fashioned in that he loved skirts and dresses, so I'd gone out and found a bunch of adorable ones. Slipping into one of them, I jumped into my car full of anticipation and left for his house. I paraded up his driveway to where he stood in the front doorway. "Like my outfit?" I crooned, beaming up at him.

Why didn't he look happy?

"Yeah, it's...nice." He looked me up and down, then looked away. "Did you already take off the tags?"

"Yeah, why?"

He was silent. I had this dreadful feeling that I'd made a horrible mistake.

"Why would you take off the tags?" his voice was too quiet. "I want to see the outfits first, to see if I like them. Remember that one time you showed me the dress before you took off the tags? I liked that. It was like you wanted my opinion, like you respected my authority."

I couldn't believe my thoughtlessness. How had I never considered such a thing?

We'd had so many talks last semester about "submission." He'd opened the well-worn pages of his Bible to 1 Corinthians 11, among other passages, and carefully explained to me the role of men and women in the church and in marriage. I had a hard time accepting some things I read, and found myself all but hating this new version I saw of the Apostle Paul. He seemed like a chauvinist. But Eric easily refuted all my arguments for why certain sections were written in a cultural context. If I wanted to date him, he made it clear that we had to be on the same page.

So I justified his rock solid arguments and stepped down from leading worship sets at my church. Eventually he gave me an ultimatum, so I even stepped down from leading the Christian group on campus. I tried to convince myself that his behavior was normal for a dating relationship, even though deep down I knew it wasn't. I was willing to give up practically anything and everything he asked me to; ready to lose myself, if that's what it took to be with him. And now here was another place I was not "submitting." I was taking the tags off of my skirts before he had the chance to veto them.

— turning off my conscience —

I could dream all day. In English class I tuned the teacher to my lowest conscious frequency, overlaying that awareness with daydreams of Eric: *Holding hands for the first time after that Newsboys concert. Flowers he hand-delivered to my doorstep. The water-scented wind sweeping through my hair as we wiggled our toes in lake-side sand.* Thoroughly absorbed in the romance, I hardly noticed when Eric began molding me into the woman of his dreams.

He suggested we break up because he wasn't fully in love with me, but I fought for him to stay. It never crossed my mind that I was more valuable than that and that someday a man would love me enough to pursue me.

He flirted with the waitresses during our date nights, so I tried to lose weight, increase my makeup, and look sexier. It never occurred to me that I should wait for a man of integrity, a man who would have eyes only for me.

He bought skirts in a size two, convinced I should be able to wear them, and I lost weight. I didn't really believe that my value came from who I was as a daughter of the King, rather than what I looked like.

Nothing changed overnight, but as the weeks and months passed, I stopped thinking for myself. I let him tell me what to believe. Mindlessly (though sometimes bitterly) I accepted his wish as my command. It was the only way to keep the peace, the only way to own his attention. In essence, neither of us was being honest. He told me what to believe, and I never disagreed, because I wanted him to like me. We were both trying to manipulate each other, both trying to get our own way. And yet, despite all this, I would gladly sleep the day away to dream of him.

One night we ventured upstairs to his bedroom. That was never meant to happen, since we were not allowed to be alone at his house. But his parents were talking downstairs, so we lingered at our stop in his room. As his hands moved over my cheeks and chin and neck, his lips brushed mine. It wasn't the first time we'd kissed, but it was the first time I let kissing go so far, let it carry me away.

> In essence, neither of us was being honest. He told me what to believe, and I never disagreed, because I wanted him to like me.

Minutes passed, each one feeling like a mere second as they piled up to nearly an hour, intensity building. I suddenly pushed him away, some alarm triggered in my mind. "Stop," I whispered. "Stop."

"What?"

"I don't think we should be doing this."

The atmosphere broke apart. He stood up and sullenly walked to the other end of the room. After a few minutes of silence, his face still turned away, he said, "Then we shouldn't be together."

I leapt up. "What?! Why?"

"We can't be together without making out, so we should break up."

"That's not what you would have done with your last girlfriend!"

He shrugged.

I hesitated, playing with the hem of my shirt. I wanted this more than anything. Wanted *him*. Loved him. I would give anything — *would* I give anything?

"It's okay," I whispered.

He looked up. "No."

"No really. Kiss me. Please. I'm sorry. Just — just don't break up with me."

He hesitated. "Maybe we *should* break up. We shouldn't be making out so much."

"No," I was on the verge of tears, begging him to cross the line I'd drawn in the sand. How quickly it was erased. "Please, no."

He walked over to me and bent down, his five o'clock shadow harsh across my cheek. I checked my tender heart at the door and decided my convictions didn't matter so much.

— as they seem —

My conscience became seared. I let him push me farther and farther physically. I gave him all my heart, mind, and almost all my body. I can't lie; I enjoyed it very much. And yet inside, this habitual sin was ripping into my soul, making me numb.

Though I yearned for the washing, healing water of my relationship with God, I couldn't find my way back to the comfort and peace I'd known in His love. I knew I should break up with Eric, but I wasn't willing to do that. So I pushed God away. I went to church, played the game, did and said all the right things, *but nothing was right inside me*.

One day a guest speaker at Eric's church praised me for how godly I was based on my modest appearance. As Eric proudly held my hand in his, I looked the guest speaker in the eye and thought, *If only you knew. Things are not always as they seem. Not with Eric, not with me. Inside, I am nothing like the godly woman you see.*

I died inside, a silent death.

— stranger in the mirror —

I felt ugly and unlovable. I felt like my skin was dyed yellow when I walked through the malls filled with beautiful girls — girls whom Eric turned and noticed without hesitation. He compared me with his ex-girlfriends, got excited when I lost a couple pounds, and picked out skimpy dresses for me to wear. I did it all, hoping it would make him fall in love with me, with *only me*. As if one human has the power to give another the essence of happiness. As if it was my job to keep a guy's wandering eyes.

I hated my hair, my body, but most of all, my face. If I could get skinny enough, maybe that would balance out my crooked, ugly face. I couldn't afford plastic surgery, but I could starve myself.

> As if one human has the power to give another the essence of happiness.

Jealousy ate away at me. Why did God give all these other girls beauty, but not me? It wasn't fair! What had they done to deserve this gift of all gifts? I stared at those girls Eric checked out in the malls and the models on the magazine covers. I simultaneously hated them and wished I *were* them. I dreamed of being them. What a reprieve those daydreams were, slipping away from reality to this place where I went blissfully numb, where beauty stole over me and every head turned my way.

One day I walked into the bathroom at school and looked over toward the mirror — a habit that had become second nature. Something strange happened in that moment. I hadn't recognized myself. When I looked over and caught a glimpse of the beautiful girl in the mirror, I thought bitterly, *I wish I looked like her*. Almost immediately, though, I thought, *Wait, she's wearing the same shirt as I am...* and then at last, *Wait...that's...me...?* I stared at myself until I heard the stall door open next to me. It was the first time I saw myself like a stranger would, the first time I saw beauty in my own face, *the first time*...which was too quickly forgotten.

— endings —

We courted for 16 self-righteous months. Months of slow death. Of fear. Of self-loathing.

There were moments of romance: those times when he'd pull his car off to the side of the road for a glorious sunset, or times when we'd walk hand-in-hand beneath the stars to the soft song of crickets. There had been candlelit dinners for two with waltzes playing in the background, not to mention flowers, original love songs, and kisses.

Yet every moment of romance became tainted by bitterness of heart. I was dying inside. I had become barely recognizable, from the weight I dropped physically, to the way I drove to school in a haze. The girl who once drove to school with fervent prayers now sat in foggy silence, hardly noticing where she turned, her clothes falling off her bony frame.

It should have been obvious. Sometimes it's easy for me to confuse emotions with convictions, to think that a hormonal "feeling" is actually a word from God. *But this was not one of those situations.* I felt incredibly convicted about being in this relationship. I was going way too far physically, and obsessing over him to the point of letting everything else in my life slip out of balance. Not only was it incredibly obvious that the relationship was negatively impacting every facet of my life, but mentors, parents, and friends also told me I shouldn't be with Eric. They didn't like who I was becoming. Deep down, I knew he wasn't treating me right, but I justified everything he did, and I ignored anyone who told me I should break up with him.

As my sophomore year of college drew to a close, Eric and I asked my parents' permission to marry. Dad's face went beet red. "*No way. I will never give my blessing. I cannot stop you, but I will not bless it.*"

I had to have his blessing. I begged and pleaded, but the greatest blessing he ever gave me was withholding it.

It was then I began to wake up. I woke up from what seemed to be a spell, a dream, a nightmare. I began to see that something wasn't right, and things weren't as I'd dreamed they would be.

No one would love me again, of that I was sure. I was unworthy and didn't particularly look forward to marriage anymore if all guys were like Eric, but I had to breathe again. I had to live again.

I tried to break up. Time and again I drove to his house sobbing, broke up with him, and within minutes fell into his arms as he reasoned me out of my hysteria and attributed it to PMS, no matter what time of the month. I resorted to phone calls, only to call back within hours begging forgiveness. I felt I had no willpower or strength to end it on my own.

— rescue —

My dad rescued me from the black hole. He saw me slipping and felt helpless when he'd reach for my hands and I'd yell at him to let me go. One night, he took my hands anyway to pull me out, no longer caring what my response was; only wanting to save his daughter.

Sitting at the kitchen table, I asked his opinion about Eric. Once again he told me I should break off the relationship. Once again I tried to justify it, craving his blessing. And for the first time, he began to ask pointed questions. Questions I never wanted to be asked, much less answered. Questions about how far we'd gone physically, what we had done when no one was watching.

For a brief moment I considered lying to my father, nearly too embarrassed to answer honestly, but I couldn't do it. Somewhere inside I drew up the courage, held my breath, and plunged in. The redness in my face betrayed me. I wanted to seep into the floor, to melt, to disappear.

My father picked up the phone with trembling hands and called my boyfriend. He said, "I trusted you with my daughter," and let the words hang in the air like smoke. And then, "If you ever come over again, I will call the police."

When he hung up, the relationship was over. For an instant, my heart took flight. Peace invaded the shadowy recesses of my soul, which had been captive to constant fear and nightly terrors. Joy and clarity burst into my mind. Breath came into my searing lungs.

But only for the night.

In the morning, raw grief ripped through me. It was a sorrow like I'd never known nor ever imagined. Pain that nothing but time — long, dreadful, slow-moving time — could ease. A different kind of fear overtook me: fear of being alone, of never finding or liking myself again, of ending up single forever.

I didn't think there was anything better for me. I didn't think I was worth the rescue. I didn't think someone else would love me.

> If I had looked up into my Father's eyes, not for one moment would I have feared the future.

Looking back, my heart breaks for that 18-year-old girl with her perfect smile and counterfeit laugh. If she knew her worth, she never would have tolerated a guy like Eric. If she had known the deep delight of her heavenly Father, there would have been no hesitation in ending the relationship. *If she had looked up into her Father's eyes, not for one moment would she have feared the future.*

— my choice —

Eric never again set foot in my parents' house, but he sent flowers and cards through friends, told me he had changed, and that he wanted another chance. Six weeks later the magnetic pull was too strong. My dad, in frustration, agreed to let me date him if we spent no time alone together.

After a week or two, the hint of freedom I'd tasted at the first break-up had disappeared. All I knew now was the taste of metal, of familiar shackles slipping around me, a prisoner in this relationship.

One afternoon during finals week sophomore year, I slipped into a practice room, shut the door, and prayed harder than I'd ever prayed before. "God, I don't know who you are anymore, and I don't know if I even *want* to know you. *But I need your help.* I need you to help me break up with Eric and not run back to him. I don't have the strength in myself. I can't do this. I keep caving. I need you. Please! Forgive me for running; I desperately need you."

Then I dialed Eric's number. He was on vacation. I suppose interrupting his vacation to break up with him was quite a low move, but it was also the only way I could truly end our relationship. I told him I didn't think we should be together.

"Sometimes I think—" He stopped his thought. After I begged to hear the rest, he finished, "Sometimes I think you're worthless."

"Then that's the end." I hung up and cried.

— like yesterday —

In all my life, I've never known a power like love, a force of such passion and fury, with the ability to bring the deepest joy I've imagined, but also to bring the deepest, most searing pain.

Ten years ago I stepped across the threshold of no return, yet I remember it like it was yesterday. Every detail is imprinted on my mind. It's not good or bad, doesn't make me particularly happy or sad, it just *is*; like one of those defining life moments that will always be there. His hands on my waist. The expressions of his eyes. The timbre of his voice. The way my heart twisted in two at his harsh words.

I remember everything like it was *just yesterday*.

BOY TALK

RECOGNIZING HEALTHY RELATIONSHIPS

If you're anything like me, you've heard 1,938,045 things you should look for in a boyfriend or future husband. And yet so many of those things have little or nothing to do with a guy's character. Here are some things I've learned over the past few years, which I hope will be practical ways you can see if your relationships are healthy:

1) Date someone who shares your faith. The Bible says we should only date and marry people who share our faith,[3] and that makes sense. If my relationship with God is truly the most important part of my life, and if it influences all my decisions, then someone who doesn't share that priority will never "get me" at the core. Besides, if I truly love God, I'll obey the instructions in His word.[4] But dating someone who shares our faith is just the minimal requirement. *Just because a guy's a Christian, doesn't mean he's not crazy!!* As my mom would say, church is full of broken people; we're all in different places along life's journey. Just because a guy's a Christian doesn't mean he has reached a point in his journey where he has character, work ethic, or integrity. And just

---

[3] *See 2 Corinthians 6:14.*

[4] *See John 14:15.*

because he's a good guy doesn't automatically mean he's right for you. So what else do you look for? Read on!

2) Look at what truly matters. Oh yes, I made a list of all the things I wanted in my future husband. They were the *truly important* things like being 6'3" tall, playing guitar, leading worship, being a youth leader, and having the name Eric.[5] Only I discovered that those things actually don't matter at all — *not one bit*!! Involvement in any ministry, leading worship from the stage, and even well-worn Bible pages guarantee *nothing* in a person's character! It's things like work ethic, integrity, consistency, humility, and willingness to learn that speak to a person's character.

3) Take things slow. And by this I mean don't talk about the "m" word ("marriage!") from the get-go. Just get to know the guy! *Especially* if you're in your teens. Most of the time the first guy you date will not be the guy you marry, and that's okay! If I hadn't been so marriage-focused from the beginning, this relationship with Eric wouldn't have been half as devastating. Don't get trapped in a bad relationship just because he's the first guy you dated. Don't get super marriage-focused or physical from the beginning. Instead, date to learn about yourself and others. Have fun, be safe, and be wise. Don't move too far or too fast in your mind, heart, *or* body. As one of my mentors likes to say, time is your friend. So take your time before getting serious with a guy.

4) Date in community. I was one of those girls who got a boyfriend and disappeared off the face of the earth. I quit my youth group, worship team, and all the other activities I did with people who had known me for years. That was one of the dumbest things I've ever done. If your boyfriend tries to take you away from your friends and family, or tries to decide who you can be friends with, I have one word of advice for you: *RUN!* Isolation is one of the first signs of harmful relationships, because it makes a person feel like they have no one to turn to but their partner, which makes

---

[5] *Names have been changed to protect the innocent. And the not-so-innocent.*

them vulnerable to being hurt. The most important thing I've learned is this: *Date in community.* That means staying close with the adults you admire and trust, letting them speak into your life, and listening if they have concerns with your relationship. It means hanging out in groups with your friends, so they can get to know you and your significant other as a couple, to see if you are good together. Love is blinding in its brilliance, and sometimes it takes someone else — someone who knows and cares for us — to see when something is out of place in a relationship.

5) Ask for advice from older and wiser people. Who are the adults in your life that are admirable, wise, and trustworthy? Maybe it's your parents, youth leaders, or a friend's parents. Think of people who are older and wiser than your peers, people who know you well, and who have your best interests in mind. Okay, what do those people think of your relationship? I used to think that was a scary question. *But it shouldn't be.* It should, in fact, be a comforting question, a place of safety for us when we listen to their advice.[6] In the same way, if the person you're dating is unwilling to listen to advice or correction, or is unwilling to respect the authority in your life (particularly your parents), that's a huge warning sign!

6) Encourage rather than manipulate each other. If your boyfriend is trying to control or dictate your decisions, something needs to change. In the same way, we must be careful not to control, guilt-trip, or use that magical pout we've perfected in the mirror (*c'mon, I know I'm not the only one!*) to manipulate someone else into becoming or giving what we want. A strong relationship is one in which both people can grow closer to God and more like Him, encouraging each other on that journey, without trying "play God" by attempting to change the other person ourselves.

---

[6] *See Proverbs 11:14.*

7) Keep your relationship in balance. Did you ever read Twilight[7] (back when it was semi-cool)? Remember how the author included something like 248 blank pages of Bella's heartbroken state when Edward left? (Okay, I'm exaggerating.) I love that God gave us the ability to be so excited about a relationship that it becomes larger than life, but when it swings out of balance with the rest of life (like it did for Bella), that's when we need to be careful. So often we lose ourselves in relationships, putting all our eggs in one basket, and then feel completely lost when the relationship ends. How do we prevent this? Stay close with your friends (as we've said). Keep doing the things you love doing, developing your interests and passions (i.e. sports, music, hobbies). Have things you do on your own or with friends, so that your whole world isn't immediately wrapped up in a boy. And above all else, *stay close to Christ*. If we're looking to a significant other for happiness or purpose in life, we'll never find it. No person can make us happy or totally erase loneliness from our lives. I know it sounds cliché, but the Creator of the human heart is the only One who truly knows how to fill it. It's normal and beautiful to feel giddy with delight when you've found a great guy. It's normal to find your thoughts flitting to him over and over, but do you enjoy it with God, or do you enjoy it apart from God? Do you surrender the relationship to God, whatever that may mean, or do you try to hold *onto it* instead of holding onto *Christ*? When I'm in a relationship and begin to feel super needy toward the guy, it's a sign that my relationship may be out of balance. I have to get on my knees and ask God to fill the needs in my heart that only He can fill.

> Do you enjoy the relationship apart from God, or do you enjoy it with God?

---

[7] Stephenie Meyer, *Twilight* (New York, NY: Time Warner Book Group, 2011).

DISCUSSION QUESTIONS

Use these questions as part of a small group, with a mentor, or on your own. As you prayerfully reflect on these, feel free to journal your thoughts in the spaces below each question.

1) What was the first warning sign you noticed in my relationship with Eric? Have you ever seen that warning sign in one of your relationships?

_____

_____

_____

_____

2) After reading the tips on recognizing healthy relationships, what other signs would you add to that list — signs that can help you know whether or not a relationship is healthy?

_____

_____

_____

_____

3) The greatest blessing my dad ever gave me was withholding his blessing from my relationship with Eric. Think about the adults in your life who know you, the adults you care about getting their blessing. Have you ever discovered that their "no" was actually a blessing in disguise? What was that like? How do you currently respond when they have concerns about a relationship you're in?

_____

_____

_____

_____

4) Have you ever spent so much time dreaming about a guy, that you're not sure who he actually is, as opposed to who you've imagined him to be? How can you get to know a guy for who he is rather than who you dream him to be?

_____

_____

_____

_____

5) Was there anything else that stuck out to you in this chapter?

_____

_____

2 THE RUNNING YEAR

AGE: 17 18 19 20 21 22 23 24 25 26

I failed.

All my life, one long string of failures, and now I had one more to add to the list: I went too far physically and then didn't marry the first guy I dated and loved. Now at age 19, I was still ring-less, not in China, and also very much alive. (I guess not being martyred was the only good news so far.)

I tried to drown my loneliness that summer in the drinks of lust and seduction. Dressing in sexy outfits that practically screamed for guys to drink in the sight of my legs and body, I never asked those men to look deeper, to see who I really was. Wanting someone to know me as a person didn't feel safe; then they'd end up leaving me. Savoring their gaze, I layered flirtation like syrup onto my words and actions, and became addicted to the bittersweet game of turning a guy's head, capturing his gaze, wanting him to want me.

It all made me feel powerful and safe, somehow, from the dangers of love. If a guy noticed and wanted me, I won. The high of gaining his attention shot through my blood like a drug. But if no one noticed me, or if someone lost interest, then I lost. Then I'd step on the scale and tell myself the number I saw made me unlovable. It was just my weight.

Numbers I could fix; at least it wasn't a problem with *me*. Or so I told myself, although my heart didn't always agree.

— love affair —

Weeks passed and the lazy month of August emerged, full of anticipation and dread for the new school year. If summer were a person, that day it would have been me, sporting pastel pink pants with a lacy white blouse and, of course, a pink and white summer scarf tying it together. Cross-legged in a restaurant booth where I was meeting my friend Austin, I'd already ordered a hot fudge sundae so as not to create an awkward dance of determining who would foot the bill.

My eyes were magnetized to the mirror on my right, every few seconds pulling back toward it, scrutinizing myself. Blonde hair, blue eyes, skin tanned from lifeguarding all summer. I looked pretty good that day. Of course, there was the stomach issue. Never thin enough, but nevertheless, better than usual. Satisfactory for the day.

When Eric and I broke up, I rebounded, immediately falling head over heels with a love interest I'd been considering for the past year.[8]

Night and day, this love consumed my thoughts and dreams. It haunted me, controlled me, promised illusions of great things, and promised to take away the shame, but in the end it broke me.

Its name? *Beauty*. But it had many nicknames: Thin, Skinny, and Good Enough, to name a few.[9]

---

[8] *Some parts in this "Love Affair" section were first released on the Girls Living 4 God (GL4G) blog, and edited by GL4G's Founder Dechari Cole.*

[9] *To hear more about my journey through body image and disordered eating struggles, along with tips that helped me overcome an obsession with physical perfection, see my first book:* The Insatiable Quest for Beauty.

Beauty promised to make me good enough, to make men like Eric fall in love with me, to give me an intoxicating kind of power. And I believed every single lie.

I'd never been fully content with myself. Even now I could see the flaws in the magnetic mirror beside me: Face too long, stomach too curvy, even my sense of humor too dull. These insecurities attacked me every moment of every day, leaving me in tears at night, begging God to make me beautiful.

When Eric and I broke up, my struggle with disordered eating nearly swallowed me whole. I lost far too much weight, but never enough to please Beauty. I got a new wardrobe, which was nice until I went out in public and saw what the "truly beautiful" girls were wearing. I was willing to do anything to make Beauty happy, and I did things that hurt my body. Things I never thought I would do, not in a million years.

And yet none of it worked. The further I fell into the affair, the more broken I became. I lost myself so completely that I had no idea who I was anymore. Nor did I know who God was. All I knew was the perfect façade I wore at all times, the mask I wanted people to see of the girl who had it all together.

But that mask wasn't me. And I hated myself for that. Hated the person I'd become.

I thought back on just a few days before, when Eric and I met up one last time. Looking over as if seeing me for the first time, he'd said sadly, "Tiff, you've gotten too thin! You need to gain some weight!" The feeling was *utter triumph.*

I replayed that moment continually before my eyes, dreaming of yet another similar encounter. A day when I would be ten pounds thinner and he would see me again. The horror registering on his face. The downcast realization of what he'd missed out on. *And that thirst was destroying me.*

The bells on the ice cream shop door jingled, jolting me from the mirror-induced trance as Austin strode in.

Oh yeah, I forgot to introduce Austin. I met him through Eric at community college. Though Austin worked there, he was only a few years older than me. The first time I met him, it was like the shock of cold water on a hot day. *Those eyes!* Not milk chocolate, but blue as the sky. Girls constantly asked me to set them up with him, but they only saw his outside. He was cute, sure, but he deserved a really great girl.

Since he advised the Christian club on campus, we got to know each other. On a few occasions he double dated with Eric and I. On more occasions I lounged on the couch in his office, chattering away when he really needed to be doing work.

So when Eric and I broke up, Austin had seen the whole thing. *He knew.* And he became a refuge for me.

When his eyes landed on me there in the ice cream shop, he nodded and ambled over. "Hey, how's it goin'?" he asked, looking up as the waitress handed him a menu. "Thanks," and then to me, "What are you getting?"

"Oh, I got an ice cream sundae. I already ordered," I waved away the question, a beehive thumping around in my stomach.

"Oh really? You're not getting lunch?" he looked at me suspiciously.

"Not hungry." That was true. "Already ate." Not entirely true. But hey, I'd be eating a sundae, wouldn't I?

"Okay," he didn't look convinced. "Well I know what I want. I'll take this one." The waitress nodded, taking back the menu. "How are you?" he asked, eyes boring into me.

"I'm good thanks!" I was bubbles and air that day, the embodiment of summer. Partly because sitting there with Austin made me feel that way and partly because of my ceaseless charade. It was the girl I thought guys wanted me to be.

I'd spent the summer building relationships with guys I called my friends, though none of them really were. How *could* they be, when they only saw the façade? *Bubbly and not-that-smart.* I hid my deepest dreams of working with young women, hid my high GPA, hid my deep emotions. They wouldn't like me if they saw those things. I'd rather have shallow friendships than rejection. Plus, if they rejected me, it wouldn't really be *me* that they rejected.

"You must be excited to transfer! You're gettin' old, Tiff. When do you move out to Rochester?"

"This weekend!" I drew a deep breath. "I can't wait to get away."

— haunting memories —

Every street, highway, mall, and restaurant was frequented by memories, trapping me in all the moments Eric and I had shared. A desperate urge to escape welled up inside me. If I could get far enough away, surely I would snap out of this living nightmare. The chaos within me would morph into peace. I could break up with Beauty just like I'd left Eric.

Although I'd been accepted to a local college in my hometown of Albany, NY, I decided last minute to transfer. School shopping began in earnest, preferably for a southern school without winters, but in the last minute rush, Roberts Wesleyan College, a Christian school in Rochester, NY (four hours west of Albany), turned out to be the most practical.

Excitement blossomed within me as I planned a last minute goodbye party, packed my dorm room supplies, and stared into the mirror wishing away any "excess" pounds.

I'm getting away! My thoughts leapt with joy. *Away from it all, and my issues will disappear. I'll be normal again!*

— just friends —

Austin's food came out with my sundae. There was always room for ice cream in my world. If it was the only thing I ate for dinner, I still made room for it. *My guilty pleasure.* I pounded spoonful after spoonful into my mouth, wanting to taste all of it at once, wanting it to never end.

"Have you met your roommate yet?" Austin asked, mouth full of burger.

"Yeah, we talked and she seems really nice!" I set down my spoon for the moment, willing myself to slow down. This is how I was with food. Ever since this love affair with beauty, food was all or nothing. Nowhere in-between. "I'm hoping to meet some cute guys there," I added with a giggle.

Austin grinned. "You're getting over Eric then?"

I shrugged away the question. *Getting over him??* How could I get over him when every minute of every day he came into my mind? Getting angry at him, sure. Despising him, yes. But *over* him? Not at all. Not if I was being honest with myself. "He calls me a lot wanting to hang out," I answered, "but I don't return the calls anymore."

"Good, I'm glad. You have to make a clean break. He's a nice guy, just an idiot."

I looked at him in partial disgust. Though his statement was true, it hit too close to home. Over and over, day after day, everyone who knew Eric asked me the same question: *Why'd you break up with him? He's such a nice guy!* If only they knew. Things are not always what they seem to be.

Then again, in four days I'd be gone. Away from that question.

I changed the topic. "So what are you doing this fall?"

We chattered on as minutes ticked by all too quickly. Glancing at his watch Austin groaned, "Mmm, I better be going. Gotta hit the gym before youth group."

"Are you leading Bible study tonight?"

"No, just helping out. But hey, Tiff, I wanted to ask you something."

"Sure!"

"Is it okay if we're friends? Like, *just friends*. I'd like to keep hanging out with you, but I just want to make sure we're on the same page, so I don't lead you on. Is that cool?" We headed toward the door, which he swung open for me.

I nodded, strangely disappointed. *What was that feeling? When had I ever thought we'd be more than friends?* Okay so maybe on occasion when Eric was being particularly awful I'd found myself wondering about Austin. But really, that was just my subconscious, nothing serious. "Totally fine. Thanks for clarifying, I appreciate it."

"Okay cool," he smiled, walking me to my car. "I just wanted to make sure we were on the same page, but I didn't want things to be weird. Alright, well, I'll talk to you later! Give me a call sometime and let me know how school is going."

— Kelly —

My family helped move me into my dorm room. I just wanted them to leave so I could be alone, but once they left I wanted them back.

I'm escaping, I'm escaping. Everything will be normal inside me now! I thought. But you can't escape from yourself.

My college RA, Kelly, bounded into my room, reddish blonde hair pulled into a ponytail. "Hey, you must be Tiffany!" I could make out a slight Canadian accent. "I'm your RA — another student on the floor that's here to be a resource to you. You're a transfer student, right? Where are you from?"

She was so pretty, so kind, so peppy. Exactly the person I wanted to be. *Watch, there's going to be a ring on her finger*, I thought, trying to distinguish her ring finger as her hands flew around. *No ring? Then at least a serious relationship. No way someone like that is single.* In my mind, being single meant something was wrong with me. If I was truly good enough, I'd be snatched up in a heartbeat by the man of my dreams. So certainly Kelly must be taken.

"Yeah, I went to a community college back in the Albany area. I'm so excited to be here though and living on campus! I'm hoping there are some cute guys? My boyfriend and I just broke up."

She threw back her head and laughed kindly. "Yeah, there are some cute guys. I'm not dating anyone though. I kind of go by this idea of 'fall asleep in Jesus and He'll wake me up when the right guy comes.'"

Come again? What kind of life philosophy was that?? Um, pretty sure if you fall asleep you'll miss them all! I wanted to say. *And how could you be okay to fall asleep?* I couldn't even *physically* fall asleep, I was so lonely!

"But there are cute guys here," she continued, bubbling grace and life all over my room. "I take it your favorite color is pink?" she observed from the decorations.

"Totally. I haven't finished decorating yet. I'm waiting for my roommate to see which bed she wants."

"Well if you need anything, let me know. I'm just down the hall. It was really great to meet you!"

I watched her go, wondering again how she could be so happy being all alone.

— parade of boys —

The first few weeks at my new college, I kept busy with dates, girls' nights, and making friends. That is, if you could call them friends, since no one knew the real me.

I could become whoever I wanted to become. There were no expectations, and I was so busy that I didn't have time to face my true self. I could hide behind whatever persona I created. Try to hide from myself and from the shame.

And yet, *what loneliness*, when I sat down and realized none of my friends knew any of the struggles that consumed my mind. And I wasn't about to tell them.

If only something good could come from my relationship with Eric, but I knew that was a useless question to ask. All the dreams I'd had in life, all the ways I'd hoped God would use me, *gone*. Just like that. One huge mistake and my life was forever scarred.

I told my mom that I felt ruined, like I'd messed up too badly for God to work in my life again. She said to wait and see what God would do with my mistakes, but I couldn't believe her at the time. I thought my brokenness and shame were too big for even God to turn into beauty.

Thus began the parade of boys, starting my first weekend on campus. Two guys asked me to hang out that Saturday, and I figured I could fit them both in if I just timed it right (which, being a bit OCD with my planner, seemed perfectly doable). Into my schedule it went: Guy number one during the afternoon, guy number two at the evening concert. It was working perfectly until Guy One insisted he should walk me over to the concert, seeing as it was getting dark out. I insisted he did not need to walk me as it was, in fact, *not* dark yet. He insisted he must play the gentleman. Play the gentleman he did, walking me right up to my evening date. I introduced the two, and upon seeing the expressions on their faces, fled the scene on the pretense of finding a snack. The two became fast friends. True story.

I always had to have a few guys interested in me, the more the better for my ego. I also had to keep them on this leash where I led them on enough to maintain the interest, but never actually dated them or admitted my interest in them to anyone else. Why? There were a couple reasons.

First, if they dumped me, I didn't want anyone to think I was a failure. *Anyone besides myself, that is.* I couldn't be seen as a girl who couldn't keep a guy's attention, because that was too close to the truth. So I kept everyone at arm's length. Close enough to seem like someone who could get a guy's attention, but far enough away that no one would think I was trying to keep it.

And don't forget, these love interests had to be *hot*. No short guys or weird faces or less-than-sculpted bodies. I was thoroughly blind to my hypocrisy, blinded with anger at the way guys expected girls to be perfect, even as I was placing the same expectations back onto them. Little did I know, I was treating them the same way I hated being treated, possibly worse.

Second, I was *so scared*. Can I say that again in huge, bold font? I was **SO SCARED**. Terrified, really. I thought deep down that every guy would treat me like Eric had, and had no idea how to be vulnerable or fall in love again. I wanted desperately to be loved, but was too scared to let anyone get close enough to love me.

It all came down to *insecurity*. I was too insecure to date someone based on who they were as a person, rather than how they looked. Too insecure to be without a prospective boyfriend. Too insecure to actually make it official with any of those prospective boyfriends. Too insecure to risk crumbling my heart yet again with a guy who would probably leave me for someone better.

God in His infinite goodness protected me even from myself, when I didn't want His protection. Time and again, as I'd start to get involved with a guy, I felt like I was going to throw up. I don't know how else to describe it; each time I saw the guy, I felt physically ill. So I'd move on to my next lust interest, until again I felt too sick to see him anymore.

The only semi-honest relationship I had with a guy was with Austin. We talked a few times a week, and each time the conversation could carry on for multiple hours. For a phone-a-phobic person like me, that was pretty impressive.

In later years, Austin told me that during our phone calls, I would say, "No one likes me! What's wrong with me? Why doesn't anyone like me?" The following week I would complain, "These seven guys are all stalking me and I can't get rid of them! I don't know what to do!" The next week I was back to, "No one likes me." He laughed and tried to show me my inconsistencies, but I'd have none of it. The fact was, none of the super cute guys I wanted to like me seemed to stick around. They'd be interested for a hot minute and then move on, leaving me once again with the realization that I was not the kind of girl who could keep their attention.

— Adonis —

One evening I pranced out of my building in the same summer outfit I'd worn at ice cream with Austin. It was one of the few days when I felt beautiful, the days I practically killed myself for.

As I came to the entrance of my building, an absolutely riveting young man opened the door from the other side, drinking me in with his milk chocolate eyes. No, it was all in my head; there was no way this Adonis[10] could be interested in me, so I kept walking and called out my typical chipper, "Thank you SO much!"

---

[10] In Greek mythology, Adonis is the god of beauty and desire, so it seemed an apt nickname for this young man.

He grinned and teased, "You're welcome SO much!"

It made me stop and turn around for half a second, locking eyes. No, *no way*. I was definitely not cute enough for *that* guy.

But he kept appearing, talking with me like I was the only person in a room, walking me home from classes, inviting me to watch his games. In response, I painstakingly curled my hair, strapped on heels each time I left my room, and criticized my body constantly.

But deep down, I knew it was too good to be true.

My RA Kelly found me one night. "Do you know Josh?"

Adonis, my mind translated. I was laughing in the hallway of my dorm, too busy playing happy to notice the perpetual ache inside. "We've met, but I don't really know him well." I tried not to appear too eager. *Had he mentioned me?*

"Yeah, I noticed you guys talking. He said today that if he didn't have a girlfriend he'd date you." She paused as her words sunk in, eyes filling with compassion. "I didn't say anything sooner because I wasn't sure if he was still dating someone else, but he is. I just want you to know so you don't get hurt."

There was no time for sadness. It'd been nice to feel wanted, but I definitely wasn't hurt by his actions. I was just plain old mad. That one small experience with Adonis brought all my hurt and anger with Eric to a boiling point.

Right then and there I decided that every guy I met deserved some "ego-busting," as I called it. They deserved to have their hearts broken, to have their pride bashed, to know that the world didn't revolve around them. I concluded that all guys were the same, and it was about time someone treated them the way I'd been treated. No one was exempt. Eric had proven this for all men. Adonis and the other guys I'd met who saw only my body (perhaps because that was all I showed them), confirmed my suspicions: *Guys were just plain mean.* They thought they could get whatever they wanted by leading girls on, never caring how they made girls feel. So it was time they got a taste of their own medicine. It was time a girl tried to break their hearts like they'd broken ours.

All my life I had dreamed of a man who would pursue and fight for me. A man who would say I was worth everything to him, who would win my heart and say I was good enough just as I was. Somewhere, somehow, my childlike faith had trusted God would bring us together.

After dating Eric, I became a realist. *Let's be honest.* I knew now that would never happen. Sure, I still wanted to get married, but I assumed no matter how wonderful a guy seemed on the surface, he'd end up cheating or discovering along the way that I wasn't good enough. And what would happen then?

I loved my ego-busting game. I loved leading a guy on and then disappearing from his life. Those dreams of a man who would catch me, fight for me, love me? I suppose they were still there, but pushed deep down into the blackness. I savored those dreams in quiet moments, because that was the only place this man existed.

— protect me —

Even as I began playing with guys' hearts and running from relationships out of fear and bitterness, I began to pray a new prayer. One I dreaded but knew was needed: *"Father, protect me from myself."*

Desires and longings stirred within me, the deepest, most hollow cravings for love. For relationship. To have someone hold me and tell me I was enough. I was afraid I would throw myself at the next guy who came along, whether or not he had a girlfriend, whether or not he was a Christian, whether or not he treated me right.

I didn't trust myself. In my vulnerable mindset, I would run headlong into heartache. So as much as I didn't want to pray it because I knew He would take me up on the request, I had to ask: "Lord, would you protect me from myself?"

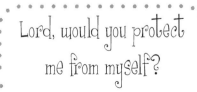

Lord, would you protect me from myself?

Looking back, I can see His Father's delight in that prayer. I couldn't hear Him then, but I'm sure He whispered, "Yes, My daughter. I will protect you. I will fight for you. I will keep you for the man I can trust with the heart of My daughter."

— wallpaper and leaves —

If only I waited. I'm single because I dated Eric when God told me not to. Just one more year, and surely I would have been married by now! The thoughts plagued me at my desk, in class, with friends. Beneath a perpetual haunting ache, I tried to decipher the reason for my prolonged singleness.

As months passed, fear gripped my heart. What if I never found *the one?* What if my disobedience in dating Eric had cost me my future? What if I would now be single forever? Should I commit to another year of singleness, since I never finished the first one? Maybe God would then bring my husband. Maybe I could manipulate the situation.

The pain overwhelmed me; loneliness took away my breath. Week after week replaced crush after crush. Guys walked in and out of my awareness, convincing me I was not the "falling in love" type of girl; I was not the kind of girl that could keep a guy's attention, not the kind of girl that someone pursued.

I numbed the ache with daydreams, imaginings that soothed my soul to sleep at night, images of a man who would pursue me and win my heart. I plastered my dorm room walls with wedding magazine photos, crafting homemade wallpaper from pictures of glamorous brides and diamond rings, creating a safe place I could escape to. Throughout monotonous days and lonely Friday nights, I'd set down my textbooks and wander around my room, slowly tracing my fingertips from photo to photo, imagining my own forever-after.

Why did I feel such a need to have a relationship? What was I trying to fill inside my heart? Looking back, I see that I felt valueless. Worthless. Lonely. Unwanted. Forgotten.

Invisible. These were the empty places of my heart that I thought could be filled by a boyfriend. I thought a ring on my finger would mean someone chose me; wanted me. And maybe for the briefest moment a guy would help fill, or at least numb, those empty places inside.

But not long-term. *Never long-term.*

Even my married friends with wonderful relationships found themselves lonely, sometimes even more than when they'd been single. There was only One place where I could find my value and worth: in the arms of a Savior. Only One who would never leave me alone. Only One who saw me and wanted me and remembered me even in my most broken moments.

At the time, I didn't understand these things. I still thought marriage would fill my heart. And so, curled up beneath the wedding pictures, I'd beg God to fill the emptiness of my heart, either taking away the intensity of these desires or sending my future husband. When nothing changed in my desires or relationship status, I'd get face-down on the floor and plead to know the future, to know how long I'd have to wait for my future husband. I wasn't so good at waiting. But no answer came.

It felt like I was crying out to a God who didn't hear me, who didn't care. During those nights backed against the mini fridge in my dorm room, bundled with knees against my chest, I had no idea what was coming. As C.S. Lewis wrote, "There are far, far better things ahead than any we leave behind."[11] It would be true for me, but it didn't feel true at the time. Instead it felt hopeless, like I would be forever trapped in the pain.

Slowly, peace was beginning to come — sweet, sweet peace — and love deeper than an ocean. But peace didn't come that night in my dorm room; it didn't come that semester; it didn't even come that junior year of college. Finding healing and hope was an infuriatingly slow and painful journey, which I hated then, but now I wouldn't trade it for the world.

What I didn't realize was this: God was far more excited about the journey than the destination. Not only

[11]C.S.Lewis, *Collected Letters* (2006).

that, but His destination was quite different than mine. His destination on this journey wasn't being healed or fixed; it was knowing Him. Healing would end up being a byproduct in my story, but it was never my journey's end. He Himself was my journey's end.

And so, although He changed nothing regarding my singleness, He began to change everything else with His love. While seemingly ignoring my pleas and questions, He answered, "*I love you. I need to be enough for you. I will fight for you.*"

> God was more excited about the journey than the destination. His destination wasn't being fixed; it was knowing Him.

If nothing else, singleness kept me on my knees. It pulled me closer to my heavenly Father than I ever would have come if I was content with my life.

Perhaps this struggle with contentment was a blessing in disguise.

Summer turned into autumn with the changing leaves; autumn morphed into winter with the sounds and smells of Thanksgiving, the crisp air, the dread of heavy lake-effect snow to come.

Each day as I crunched to classes on dying leaves bright with the beautiful colors of surrender, I found myself caught in a God-sized love story. Every twinkle of sunlight on water, every breeze that blew in the tree branches, every bird that sung its way south was a love song for me. Whispers of His love surrounded me at every turn. I basked in the glory of knowing the delight of my heavenly Father.

As much as my soul ached for human companionship — the kind that lasts a lifetime, it was being nourished by heavenly revelry — the kind that lasts for *eternity*. I began to see that my heart was already spoken for by a Father who would fight for me, a Father who would never leave me.

— write —

I pulled into my parents' driveway for Christmas break that year. As I twisted off my car's ignition, I sensed the Lord whisper to my spirit, "Start writing that book."

Years ago I'd dreamed of writing a book about beauty for teen girls. I'd even started writing it at age 15, then stopped, not knowing what to say. It hadn't been time yet.

But *now*? Now, when thoughts of food and weight consumed every second of every day? Now, when my thoughts wrapped around my pursuit of marriage, my longing to be good enough so some man would stay? Now, when I'd fallen too far for God to ever work through me again? *Now* I should write it?

It was too weird, and yet I could hardly wait to start. Night after night, dates were replaced with writing this book: pouring my soul, energy, and passion into something that made me come alive.

How beautiful that God's strength becomes perfect in the place of our weakness. How beautiful that He would choose to work through my life when I felt least ready and worthy. It's then that He receives all the glory for His work, because it's nothing we could conjure up on our own.

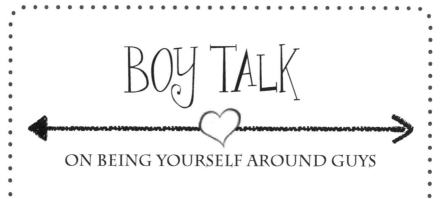

BOY TALK

ON BEING YOURSELF AROUND GUYS

While in college, I wrote a song that said: "If you saw me, would you want me? If you knew me, would you still be here? I guess I don't know." I longed to be loved, but didn't know if anyone would stick around once they saw the real me. I always wondered what would happen when they discovered I wasn't good enough.

Have you ever felt this way? Like it's hard to be your true self, especially around guys? When people told me, "Just be yourself!" I would get frustrated. Not only was I clueless how to actually be myself, but I also had no idea who that mysterious "self-person" was! Here are some things that helped me figure out who I was and how to be myself:

1) Stop looking for yourself. It seems counterintuitive, right? Don't we have to look for ourselves to find ourselves? Maybe not. I read this incredible quote by C.S. Lewis in his book <u>Mere Christianity</u> that says:

> The more we get what we now call "ourselves" out of the way and let Him take us over, the more truly ourselves we become. There is so much of Him that millions and millions of "little Christs," all different, will still be too few to express Him fully. He made them all. He invented — as an author invents characters in a novel — all the different men [and women] that you and I are intended to be. In that sense

our real selves are all waiting for us in Him. It is no good trying to "be myself" without Him... I am not, in my natural state, nearly so much of a person as I like to believe: most of what I call "me" can be very easily explained. It is when I turn to Christ, when I give myself up to His Personality, that I first begin to have a real personality of my own... Your real, new self...will not come as long as you are looking for it. It will come when you are looking for Him.[12]

I thought being myself was all about knowing my favorite colors, interests, and personality traits, and sure, that's part of being yourself in any given season. But those things change throughout life. Really, being me is about embracing the One who created me, searching the Bible for verses that tell who God has called me to be, and letting my life reflect His characteristics. Since our lives are hidden with Christ in God,[13] finding ourselves is about searching for Him. For me, that involved replacing my self-hatred with God's forgiveness for the ways I had let Eric treat me, and the ways I had devalued myself. Slowly, I let His perspective of me eclipse my own perspective. I now know who I am because I know Whose I am.

> Since our lives are hidden with Christ in God, finding ourselves is about searching for Him.

2) Experiment. Sometimes we've spent so much time trying to be who we think people want us to be, that we don't even know our favorite color! I know many girls who have so tailored their interests to the guys they like or to please others in their lives, that they no longer know what their own interests are. If that's you, begin experimenting to find things you enjoy, whether that means trying out different sports,

---

[12] C.S. Lewis, *Mere Christianity* (New York, NY: Harper Collins, 1980), 226.

[13] *See Colossians 3:1-4.*

music, hobbies, or new colors and styles of clothes. Research a new cause or check out an art exhibit; try things you wouldn't normally try! This will help you find those God-given passions that make you come alive when you do them, which in turn will help you find your place in the body of Christ.[14] Part of who I am is someone who loves meeting new people but also desperately needs time alone, someone who is passionate about girls' issues, someone who loves being girlie but also loves a crazy adventure. This probably sounds very different from the girl I wrote about in these first two chapters, and I never would have discovered these things if I hadn't experimented with new interests.

3) Thank God for making you to be you. Instead of trying to imitate someone else, thank God for the quirky personality traits and "mismatched" physical attributes that so perfectly create you. Train your eyes to see the beauty in the things that make you unique. If we all looked or acted the same, there wouldn't be anything special about us.[15]

4) Rephrase. I kind of don't even like the phrase "be yourself." It's too mysterious and it focuses too much on ourselves. As my mom has said, people were made to change so we can change to be like Christ. So instead of saying "be yourself," perhaps we should say things like, "be kind," "be compassionate," or "use your God-given gifts."

5) Guys love confidence. Okay, so being myself around guys was the hardest part of being myself. But here's what I found: Guys love confidence! It's not about being a perfect person, it's about loving life and being comfortable in your own skin. Sometimes we have to fake it until we make it, in a sense — choosing to love life and focusing on other people instead of on our insecurities. Surprisingly, the more I started being my super quirky, nerdy self, the more guys started taking notice, because I was embracing life with gusto.

---

[14] *See 1 Corinthians 12.*

[15] *For more on this topic, check out Coffee Date #5 in* The Insatiable Quest for Beauty.

When you're in high school, yes, sometimes the fake girls are the ones who get the boyfriends...but they're not the girls guys want to hang onto for the long run. If you're "yourself" in high school, you'll probably get a lot of guy friends, which is way more important at that age anyway. And if you want to be the kind of girl a guy wants to bring home to meet his mom, *be real*. In your twenties and thirties, when guys are looking for a wife, you'll find they're way more interested in girls that are real than girls that aren't, even choosing someone who's real over someone who's prettier.[16]

6) Think about play dough. Yup, the green, weird-smelling stuff you played with as a kid. Imagine God made this certain lump of green play dough. It's sitting on the counter saying, "This is me. I'm green and a lumpy circle. That's who I am." God, on the other hand, sees the creation He wants this play dough to become, so He starts squeezing and rolling it. The play dough's screaming, "Stop it! You're messing with who I am!" What the play dough doesn't realize is that it's becoming exactly who it was meant to be. Eventually it's reworked into a beautiful bowl. It's still green and it's still play dough, but it looks different, reworked into the creation God meant it to be. In the same way, being ourselves doesn't mean we never change. Here's what I mean: In our culture, we say "be true to yourself; don't change anything about you." But being yourself actually means that we are open to change, as we allow God to mold us into the person He wants us to become. We don't always know who that person is, just like the play dough didn't know it was being turned into a bowl, and that shaping process is never finished until the end of our lives. So we must ask Him for a glimpse of who He's made us to be, and the flexibility to allow Him to shape us into who He wants us to become.[17]

---

[16] *To read an interview I conducted with some guys on this topic, check out chapter eight in* The Insatiable Quest for Beauty.

[17] *See Psalm 139:13-16, Isaiah 64:8, Isaiah 29:16, Jeremiah 18:2-6, and Romans 9:20-21.*

DISCUSSION QUESTIONS

Use these questions as part of a small group, with a mentor, or on your own. As you prayerfully reflect on these, feel free to journal your thoughts in the spaces below each question.

1) Have you ever hidden your true self because you didn't think people would like you? When, and what was that like?

_____

_____

_____

_____

2) Who are the hardest people to be yourself around? For me, it was guys. What helps you be yourself in the situations where that is the hardest? What helps you around guys?

_____

_____

_____

_____

3) What do you think it means to "be yourself"? I've found it's more about becoming like Christ than about searching for ourselves. What do you think about that?

_____

_____

_____

_____

4) Have you ever rebounded for an inanimate obsession like Beauty? What was that like for you? How did you break up with that obsession?

_____

_____

_____

_____

5) Have you ever felt pressure to marry the first person you date? What does dating mean to you? How do you think dating should look?

_____

_____

_____

_____

6) Have you ever been terrified of being in a relationship? Why? What did you do?

_____

_____

_____

_____

7) Asking God to protect me from myself was scary, because I knew He'd take me up on it. Have you ever prayed something like this? What did you pray? Why? How has He answered?

_____

_____

_____

_____

3 THE SEARCHING YEAR

AGE: 17 18 19 20 21 22 23 24 25 26

Months passed. Months that felt like blank pages, with few memories. My affair with beauty turned sour. Not eating had spun out of control into binge eating. Instead of releasing me from shame, beauty had brought more shame. And yet, even in the brokenness of my relationship with food, my heart was being healed.

It's hard to explain. In part, the gradual passing of time released my heart from the rawness of memories and emotions. In the moment of a breakup, it's hard to believe you could ever be happy again, but time is truly a healing agent. However, more of the healing came from nights spent on my knees, letting my heavenly Father love me. In the stories of my Bible, in the sensation of His nearness during times of worship, in the honest friendships I was beginning to build, I sensed His love all around me. Friday nights became my "date night with God," which felt super cheesy to me, and exactly what I'd make fun of other people for doing, and yet...there I was on Friday nights. *Running to my Father.*

When I put on extra weight from binge eating — weight that stayed for a few years because I couldn't get control of my eating habits — or when fewer people asked

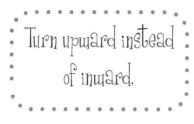

Turn upward instead of inward.

me out, I turned upward instead of inward. I found the beginning stages of healing in the truest love I could ever know. The change was so slow and subtle; I almost couldn't tell anything was changing. It was just in little things: An afternoon when I forgot I was single. A look in the mirror when I liked what I saw. Subtle, but *very real*.

Junior year turned into senior year. And then, one morning, I awoke to these words on the edge of a dream:

"The reason you're still longing for a relationship is because you're trying to win our hearts with your outward beauty," that handsome Adonis with the girlfriend was telling me. I didn't know what gave him the right to tell me such a thing, when he was the one with the girlfriend!

Bleep, bleep, bleep! *What was that sound?*

Bleep, bleep, bleep! *The sound was louder and more insistent, pushing away Adonis, and leaving behind a frantic feeling.*

Bleep, bleep, bleep!

"Tiffany, wake up!" my roommate Krysta shook me gently. "Your alarm has been going off for five minutes!"

I rubbed my eyes, confused, "He was in my dream. He was telling me I'm single because I'm trying to be beautiful."

"Huh?" now Krysta looked confused. "Who was?"

"That guy with the girlfriend. It's my fault I'm single!" The meaning of the dream dawned on me and heaviness filled me. "I have to get ready. I'm meeting Jenna for breakfast."

Krysta just stared at me, wondering if her roommate had gone crazy. "Are you okay?"

"Yeah, I'll tell you later."

Stumbling out of the bunk bed, I hurried to make up my face for the day. Each stroke of makeup reminded me of the dream. Was I still single because I was trying to win guys' hearts with outward beauty instead of inward? Was I single because I was throwing my heart at guys?

Aha! I paused in my morning routine. Many godly women had told me, "God sent my husband when I least expected it. First I had to become content being single." *That* was the issue! That's what the dream alluded to! I wasn't content.

I squinted into the mirror. *Okay, Tiffany, it's time now to become content. Stop wanting to get married! C'mon now, you want it badly enough that you can do this! The faster you become content, the faster you can get married.*

I *hated* being single. And perhaps I was single because I wasn't content, but neither were some of my friends! Many of them were in relationships, and I knew for a fact they were not okay being alone. So, why could they date when I couldn't seem to get a boyfriend? All those friends who were in relationships — what special thing did they have that I didn't? Beauty? Fashion? Popularity? Godliness?

I clacked across campus as quickly as I could manage in heels. Jenna and I were fellow RAs that year. She had half the floor and I had the other half, sixty girls between the two of us. I figured breakfast would be a great way to get to know her. Grabbing my new daily breakfast of a bagel slathered with cream cheese (which I always promised myself I wouldn't eat ever again), I shared the dream with Jenna.

"I have to learn how to be content!" I finished. "If I can finally be okay with singleness, then God will send my husband."

Jenna looked thoughtful, "But remember, Tiff, you can't fix yourself. Only God can change you. Don't be too hard on yourself; let Him do it."

Let *Him* do it? Well how long would *that* take? I didn't have a lot of time to waste, and God never seemed to be in a hurry! Here I was a senior in college, surrounded by this whole "ring by spring" fever, and I was totally single. Okay, so I didn't manage to get married by 20, but I most definitely wanted to be engaged by the end of college!

Contentment became my magic potion. If I could finally be content with what I had, I'd get what I wanted! Oh, the irony.

Be happy, be happy, be happy. You want to be single! My positive self-talk set to the rhythm of my heels didn't convince anyone, much less my heart. I definitely was *not* happy being single. It was the last thing I'd ever wanted.

— little red dress —

My senior year of college whisked by. In the midst of studying for finals and composing last minute papers, the day of the college formal came like Christmas morning.

Amidst the chaos of Black Friday, I'd found it: the dress of my dreams! Silky red fabric draped over black, knee-length crinoline. Diamonds drew the eye to an exquisitely ruched, halter-top-meets-sweetheart neckline. I'd never seen anything so perfect.

My phone rang, and I scrambled to reach it on the bathroom counter, still clutching the silky red fabric to my body. "Hey!" I managed just in time, admiring my reflection in the mirror. Red was a good color for me.

"Hey, how's it goin'?" Austin's mellow voice was nearly drowned by sounds of the highway. "I'm on my way, running about half an hour late."

He was driving four hours to take me to the formal. He'd clarified nearly a hundred times that it wasn't going to be weird, and that we'd be going as friends. I agreed, but nevertheless had a guilty bottle of cocoa walnut shell body scrub staring at me now. I glared back at its perch in the shower.

I'd just returned from a breathless dash to the corner store, having forgotten an essential detail: *I had to wear a food scent tonight!* Austin had once asked why girls didn't wear food-scented perfume if they wanted guys to like the way they smelled.

"Why not get Steak or Linguine Alfredo scent?" he'd asked.

The next time we'd traipsed through Walmart, looking for the little odd or end, I'd purchased a Peanut Butter Cup chapstick.

"Why'd you buy that?" Austin had asked. "That's kind of weird."

I stared at him. "It's a food scent!" I finally blurted. Hadn't he said girls should wear food scents?

"You don't want a guy to *eat* you, do you?" he gave me this look like I was a little kid who didn't get anything.

Undaunted, today I'd bought cocoa walnut body scrub. The smell sure was luxurious, only it had disappeared the moment I stepped out of the shower. I stared in disgust at the waste-of-money bottle, which glared back with our little secret. (At least I still had chocolate truffle perfume on my dresser.)

"Tiff?" Austin's voice snapped me out of the reverie.

"Oh! Yeah, okay! Sounds good. Park in lot K. See you when you get here!"

"Okay, see you soon!"

Shaking my head at the body scrub, I moved on to hair and makeup as my girlfriends entered our suite, chattering excitedly. "Ooh, gorgeous dress!" "Is that the one you got on Black Friday?" "Have you heard from Austin?"

Thus, the pampering party began. Thankfully I still had three hours until Austin would arrive, and every second of that time would be put to good use curling and primping. I had to look *just so*.

— perfect moment —

I definitely didn't *want* to wear a coat, but the December night was obnoxiously cold, so the black and white checkered jacket would have to be worn. At least it was classy and cute.

When Austin arrived, it took my breath away. Every girl would be jealous. Maybe, *just maybe*, he'd even kiss me tonight. When he saw me in the perfect red dress, for sure. But where did that thought come from? We were *just friends*, obviously. Or so I told myself every day, even as I found myself daydreaming of us as more than friends, and wondering how much longer it would take before he realized we were meant for each other. One day he half-jokingly asked why God still hadn't dropped his future wife into his lap, and I almost blurted out, *How much closer do I have to get?!*

He seemed a bit awkward when he arrived, not exactly sure how to handle himself. It felt so much like a date, and somewhere, deep down, oh how I wanted it to be a date! If I had a fairy godmother, that's what I'd wish for: *Make him love me!*

The night was a flurry of pictures, dancing, dinner, introductions, and laughter that tinkled like ice in goblets.

"Why don't you date him? Or him?" Austin kept whispering as he met my friends.

Seriously?! Could he not see that they were *so* not as cute as he was? "Too short," or "Not cute enough," or, simply, "Ew," were my indignant responses.

And then we were doing the lawnmower and other 80s dance moves, herded into a circle of friends bound by laughter. I felt rich and full as the night scurried on, time getting away from me. And then everything slowed down.

"I need to get some air," it was late evening when Austin announced this.

"I'll come with you." Trying not to appear too eager, the thought flashed through my mind: *Now's my chance! Surely he's hoping I follow. Maybe he wants to kiss me!*

"Okay," Austin turned to lead the way, and then on second thought asked, "Anyone else want to come?"

Please say no! You had better say no! I silently willed our table of friends.

"No, we're good," the voices said, and I exhaled quietly.

Leaving my coat on the chairs, I pretended to be overheated as well, as if it didn't bother me at all that the thin red fabric of my dress was all I had to protect me from the December wind.

We made small talk and then stood on the balcony in silence beneath the milky stars. Exactly like in my dreams: there was always a balcony when I fell in love, when I was kissed for the first time, and when I accepted a marriage proposal. *Always* a balcony.

I waited. Hugged myself against the goose bumps on my arms and the chill in my blood. I tried to look nonchalant, unsuspecting, and yet open to anything.

We stood there a few more minutes, and then Austin noticed. "Are you cold?" he asked. His jacket was inside on his seat or he would have offered it. As it was, "We should go back in, you must be freezing."

He reached for the door but I lingered, willing him with my eyes. *At least put your arm around me! Something!*

Was he uninterested or simply clueless? As if in slow motion, he pulled open the door, letting a swell of music and light intrude on the perfect moment. I followed him, rigid with cold and disappointment.

Of course he's not interested. Why would he be? No one ever is. Only in my dreams.

Krysta found me and whispered, "What happened out there?" Her eyes were bright with anticipation. "Did he kiss you?"

I shook my head. "Nothing, just got some air."

"Oh," she looked almost as disappointed as I felt.

I turned away, not wanting to cry.

— in this moment —

I uploaded all my pictures that night — all 300 of them — and turned the best into a screensaver on my old desktop computer.

Austin had left to stay with a friend who lived an hour away. I kept him company via telephone for part of his drive, pushing down my choking disappointment to help keep him awake, but now he'd arrived safely. My girlfriends were sleeping softly, and I was left to my own devices.

Pulling out my journal, I recorded every moment from the evening. Caught in contemplation, I found myself flipping idly back through the pages. The verses, the disappointments, the fears, the occasional tear stain.

My eyes were drawn to an entry from a few months prior. Psalm 37:3-4 was scrawled across the top in my messy cursive font, and then, "Trust in the Lord, and do good; dwell in the land, and feed on His faithfulness. Delight yourself also in the Lord, and He shall give you the desires of your heart."

This is it! I thought. *The key to contentment is living fully in the moment wherever God has put us (dwelling in the land), meanwhile finding sustenance and courage in the memory of His past faithfulness (feeding on His faithfulness). Instead of wishing away my present singleness, instead of numbing myself with daydreams, I am supposed to be fully present in each moment. I should take courage, knowing how faithful He's been in my life, and trusting that He will be faithful again. And then, one day, He will give me the desires of my heart.*

But there was more, I sensed it. What was there that I couldn't yet put my finger on? It was on the tip of my tongue! And then it came: *As I delighted in Him, He would become my greatest desire.* Above all other longings, my heart would crave Him first and foremost.

So this was the secret. I desperately wanted to be content, but felt guilty that I couldn't force contentment upon myself, and yet I hadn't even known what contentment was! Contentment wasn't a magic potion to get what I wanted. Nor was it losing my desire and hope for the future. Instead, it was choosing His way over mine.

How? By dwelling in the land and feeding on His faithfulness. In other words: Trusting Him enough to surrender to His way instead of mine...even if I didn't know what His way looked like just yet.

> Contentment wasn't a magic potion, nor was it losing hope for the future. Instead, it was choosing His way over mine.

A burst of December wind through the cracked window brought me back to the present. I shivered, closed my journal, and crawled into bed.

It's like those dying autumn leaves! The pre-sleep thought was like a lullaby, like the scent of cookies baking.

The leaves that become exponentially more beautiful in their surrender; that let go of their hold on the branches and slip into the most glorious release. Maybe as I surrendered to His way, without any strings attached, God would transform my brokenness into beauty. Maybe He'd make me beautiful like the leaves, with the kind of beauty that pulls your eyes heavenward. Not the kind of beauty I'd been chasing this whole time that would pull eyes to me, but the kind of glory that speaks of heaven. And that kind of beauty is just like contentment; it only comes from surrendering all to Him, letting go, like the leaves are letting go of the branches, so I can fall into Him.

REFLECTIONS ON CONTENTMENT

Growing up in church, this is the advice I've heard time and again: "Once I became content, God sent my husband to me." Which to me seems weird, because then we think, "Okay, if I can just become content, I'll finally get what I want!" And isn't that the opposite of contentment? Here are some things I've been learning recently:

1) Contentment is not a magic potion. It's not a way to get what we want. It's not a formula to change our circumstances.

2) Contentment is a surrendered state of heart. It's choosing joy and surrendering our desires, even when our circumstances don't feel very good.

3) Contentment is not an excuse. It's easy to hide behind an idea of contentment, sounding very spiritual when we say we don't need anyone in our lives, even as we crave that with all our soul. It's not an excuse to stay home and safely, yet passively, do nothing when we could be out building relationships, pursuing our dreams, and possibly even meeting that special someone.

4) Contentment is a choice. It's not a magical moment when our emotions line up with our minds or spirits. It has nothing to do with a change in circumstances or feelings. (Especially as women, our feelings will change every day with our hormones and therefore, are not a good thermostat for our spiritual health.) Rather, contentment is a lifestyle that we *choose* — choosing to trust God instead of trying to manipulate Him into changing our circumstances.

5) Contentment doesn't always feel content. In Philippians 4:11-13, Paul writes, "I have learned in whatever state I am, to be content...to be full and to be hungry, both to abound and to suffer need. I can do all things through Christ who strengthens me." Hunger is an in-your-face desire. You can't forget you're hungry. Yet Paul was content while he was hungry; he didn't cease to become hungry once he became content. Singleness too is an in-your-face desire. You don't forget you're single. So if Paul could be content while he was hungry, then I can be content even while aching for a happily ever after (preferably involving a balcony).

6) We can be content in every season of life. God has been teaching me recently that every season of life shares the same goal: To love God and love others. Whether we're married or single, rich or poor, whole or broken, we can be moving toward that same goal of loving and being loved by God more fully. Contentment has nothing to do with a change in our circumstances; it has everything to do with the position of our hearts.

> Contentment has nothing to do with a change in our circumstances. It has everything to do with the position of our hearts.

DISCUSSION QUESTIONS

Use these questions as part of a small group, with a mentor, or on your own. As you prayerfully reflect on these, feel free to journal your thoughts in the spaces below each question.

1) How would you define contentment? Have you ever thought of it like a magic potion? How does Philippians 4:11-13 impact your understanding of it?

_____

_____

_____

_____

2) Are you pursuing the kind of beauty that pulls eyes heavenward, or that pulls eyes to you? How can you tell the difference?

_____

_____

_____

_____

3) How can you live fully present in the season you've been given right now? In this season, how can you learn to love God and love others more fully?

_____

_____

_____

_____

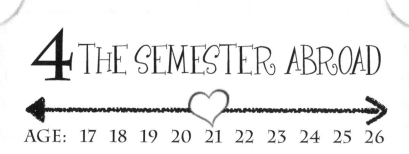

4 THE SEMESTER ABROAD

AGE: 17 18 19 20 21 22 23 24 25 26

I stepped off the plane and took in the city surrounding me. *Sydney.*

It didn't feel real yet. *When would it feel real?* I had just set foot on Australian soil; I should be freaking out right now! I pinched myself a few times...and still, *nothing.*

If you want to get away from everything and everyone you know, you can't get much farther than the other side of the world. Hence, studying abroad in Australia with my friend (and former fellow RA) Jenna.

After another flight and a bus ride further inland, I ended up in a little town about 20 hours from Sydney. Groggy from jet lag two mornings later, I forced my feet onto the cold floor and shoved away the warm covers by sheer willpower. I dressed in the only warm outfit I'd brought. I hadn't expected Australia to get so cold!

As much as I'd found traces of healing in my relationship with Christ, I also found other desires churning within me. Leftover desires from Eric and Beauty. On the one hand, I wanted to love God with all my heart. On the other hand, I craved a glamorous Hollywood lifestyle. I was tired of the hypocrisy within me and felt that if I were ever to move forward, I had to try that lifestyle, just once: *Dating around, going dancing each weekend, having the perfect beach body, being a popular girl.* Not that there's anything inherently wrong with those desires, but I felt like I couldn't explore them until I got away from everyone who had so many expectations for me. From being an RA at a Christian college, to leading Bible studies, to being a part of my conservative family, I felt pressure to be the perfect Christian girl. Whether everyone really did have expectations or it was all in my head, I'm still not sure. But either way, I wanted to go somewhere to make my own choices — my own mistakes, if need be. So I jumped onto the "what happens in Australia, stays in Australia" bandwagon (forgetting that Facebook photos were one way in which my actions wouldn't just *stay in Australia*).

My desires scared me just as much as they excited me; I knew running away to make mistakes was not exactly a wise idea. For the past few months I'd been asking God to protect me from myself and help me to see this romanticized lifestyle the way He saw it.

Priority number one was finding a church immediately, somewhere that would keep me from going off the deep end. Sunday morning I was filled with anticipation and butterflies in my stomach. Signs had been posted for a city-wide church with several campuses, one of which met right there at my college.

It was love at first sight.

Stepping into the church, my gaze wandered around the auditorium, slowly absorbing every detail. *The hard-backed seats: each row a step up from the one behind it. The video loop projected onto the wall ahead. The stage far below with laughing musicians.* My eyes connected with the drummer. After holding his gaze for a second, I quickly looked away, not wanting to appear too interested.

When worship began, my soul was moved to the core, hungering and thirsting for more. I never wanted to leave that place.

After service I was greeted and introduced around to other people my age. The drummer in particular walked over to talk. He was sort of cute, but not my type.

No, you don't understand. He was not *at all* my type. Short with red hair? *Nope. No, thank you.*

However, I did discover he was the young adults' pastor, which was a great connection. Then I could meet all the cute guys my age! So I said hello quickly, found the young adult service times, then made my way subtly toward a cute guy chatting in the corner. By that point I couldn't even remember the red head's name. Weird.

That Sunday, I fell in love. It was the second time I'd fallen so hard and fast; only this time a boy was not involved. It was the church that made me feel like I'd come home.

— God in a bar —

My first few Australian weeks were filled with making friends, spending time with a certain cute boy with a delicious accent who I'd met at the college (no, no, different boy, not the red head), shopping, clubbing, and dragging myself out of bed on Sunday mornings because I couldn't bear to miss a week of my new church.

One particularly memorable clubbing expedition came five Saturdays into my time abroad, as fifty international students clambered onto a school bus for a trip to the Gold Coast. Promises and illusions of Hollywood moments danced before my eyes, as the flat, barren scenery blended into the background.

Arriving at the hostel, several of us purchased tickets for a "bar crawl," our opportunity to explore the glamorous clubs along the coast. Excitedly I changed into a brand new outfit: White shorts with leggings, sparkly red Dorothy-style flats, and a matching red sweater. With honey blonde hair setting off tanned skin and blue eyes, I felt like the Barbie that fellow clubbers told me I resembled.

Delicious appetizers followed the first, second, and third shots I'd ever done in my life. By the fourth bar, a quiet table and chairs off to the side seemed most welcoming. I held onto the table's edges, trying to squelch the dizziness.

"Let's get couples up here! Guys, find a lady and bring her on up!" the emcee announced. Someone tried to pull me up, but I declined for fear of falling. (Honestly, I was ready to go to bed. Late nights were not my thing.)

"Okay here are the rules," the emcee continued. "Each round you have to take one piece of clothing off your partner. Whoever sticks it out the longest wins!"

Hoots and hollers resounded as guys crowded the floor. *Thank God I didn't go up!* I thought. *It would have been embarrassing to walk off now.*

Round after round continued, and I found myself watching the onlookers more than the dancers. The glint in their eyes as guys stared unashamedly — not at the girls, but at the bodies. Never caring about the person that body housed, only digesting the images of shoulders, legs, torsos… I found myself repulsed by such animalistic lust.

Suddenly the presence of God entered the bar and washed over me. I will never forget that moment when God met me in the bar. He whispered to my spirit, in that inaudible but oh-so-clear voice of His, "Why would you pay to put yourself in this situation, when this is exactly what I died to free you from?"

Breathing a ragged breath, I saw in my mind's eye Jesus hanging on a cross. I saw the pain He'd been through, and my spirit became so grieved that it physically hurt me. His presence became more real than the pulsating music. I had to get some air.

Clinging to the wall, I made my way out onto the street. Lights and music behind and in front of me seemed a distant reality as I held my arms around my waist and nearly cried. I saw the truth. I saw what He saw, not what I'd seen.

I saw girls who were looking for love but only finding lust. Girls who pretended commitment didn't matter because they didn't want to be disappointed. Girls who flaunted their bodies hoping to gain confidence, but only finding an insatiable quest for attention.

This romanticized Hollywood lifestyle was nothing I wanted. In that moment, *I knew He'd paid with His life so that I could know true love*[18], and not have to look for it in places that would leave me broken.

---

[18] *The truest love of all comes from Christ Himself. (See John 15:13, 1 John 3:16, and 1 John 4:19, among many other passages.)*

I followed my friends to the final club before successfully begging one of them to accompany me home. As I waited, I wearily climbed onto a barstool, winding my legs through the rungs to hold up the lead they seemed to contain. When everything began moving, I assumed it was just my head spinning from too little to eat. Then I hit the floor.

Trying to untangle my legs from the stool felt like a jigsaw puzzle. A friend turned around to talk to me and didn't see where I'd fallen. He finally looked down and jumped when he saw me in the middle of the floor. I was too tired to explain; I just wanted him to help me up so I could go home.

> He paid with His life so that I could know true love, and not have to look for it in places that would leave me broken.

— being me —

After that bar crawl, I plugged in full force at my church. They became my lifeline. Anything they needed volunteers for — *hello, pick me!* As long as I could scoop up a ride (which wasn't hard to do), I'd be there.

And that's when Karl stole away my friendship by surprise. (Yep, I found out his name. The short red head.) As I got to know him, he invited me and Jenna to hang out with his group of friends at church, and particularly his best friend Mike.

I didn't expect anything more than an acquaintance. I still had a hard time building genuine friendships with guys; I felt so awkward and fake, always trying to be the girl I thought they'd want (aka, the real-life version of a Stepford wife: A girl with no dreams or interests, few brains, and flawless makeup). Even though I didn't want to be that girl anymore, I involuntarily slipped back into that act every time I was with a guy. And yet with Karl, I found myself letting go without ever realizing it.

Jenna constantly encouraged me to "just be yourself!" (Which at first was frustrating to me, because it was so much easier said than done!) However, I started acting crazier, nuttier, and quirkier. I bought bolder clothing, sassed back when people teased me, and dyed my hair bright, Ronald McDonald red. Maybe the red hair was a little overdone, but I was like a pendulum swinging the opposite direction before balancing out as *me*.

One night after a young adults meeting, ten of us crammed into Mike's living room. The foyer held a small upright piano, so of course I scrambled over to tinker on it until the rest of the group arrived. Karl walked in, promptly shoving me over on the bench to sit beside me. "Whatcha playin', Tiff? Is this one you wrote?"

"It's one I'm working on," I grinned.

"Let's hear it!"

When we made our way into the living room, someone asked, "What did you all think of the message tonight?"

It had been a message about the dreams God put in our hearts. Honestly, it had made me cringe. *Who needed dreams? I was supposed to delight in God, not in my dreams!* And then I felt God correcting me: "Tiffany, you said you want to learn everything you can from people who think differently than you. So why aren't you listening?" Maybe He wanted to teach me something about dreaming.

Each person started to share his or her dreams in life, moving around in a slow circle. I was the last to share, and hesitated. *What would they think of me? Would it sound stuck up? More importantly, would the guys be intimidated? Should I be brutally honest?*

"Well, I write music, as you guys know."

"Yeah, and we want you to play one of your songs at an event next month!" Karl added.

"I'd love to!" I stopped and stared at the floor. *Okay, let's do this. I'm being me.* "Well, to be totally honest, and I don't mean this to sound weird...but I want to preach all over the world. And write books. And I'm writing one now about body image. And I want to lead worship and see millions of lives changed."

It was quiet for a brief second that felt like an eternity. *Why did I just admit to all that?*

"And you're going to do those things," Karl broke the silence. "I have no doubt."

— denial —

"What do you think — this shirt, or this shirt?" I clutched the two options to my chest, looking from one to the other.

"I like that one," Jenna pointed to the bolder option.

"Me too," Amanda nodded.

I turned back toward the mirror, holding up the shirts for one final, deciding glance.

"I take it you're excited to see Karl again?" Amanda winked slyly.

"No!" I whirled around. "I mean, yes, but not like that. I don't like him!"

"Then why are you so worried about what you'll wear tonight?" Jenna's blonde curls bounced as she plopped onto my bed.

"I'm not! I just — you never know who you'll meet at the mall. It's not him. It's just — I'm always like this when I go to the mall."

"Tiff, you're in denial," she retorted.

I was. Hardcore denial as I shook my head, "He's way too short for me! No way."

But I couldn't wait until he picked me up, and found myself strangely disappointed when I discovered a couple other friends from church would be joining us.

"Tiff, do you think Karl likes you?" Jenna asked.

"Yeah, I think so."

"Do you think every guy likes you?"

Where was this going? "No, why?" I looked confused.

"Sometimes it seems like you do."

I stood there in disbelief. Was it not obvious that Karl liked me? As my heart grew offended, my mind flitted back.

Usually I *didn't* think guys would ever like me! How could I come across the complete opposite way?

"I don't think you mean to come across that way," Amanda added, staring at my rigid back.

"Right, I don't think it's on purpose or that you even realize it," Jenna explained. "But it does seem like you think every guy likes you, and that can be annoying."

She's right! I hated that she was right. My words *did* come across that way! But really, it came across that way because I felt insecure and not good enough. So if I talked about all the guys that liked me, it would make me feel better about myself. I had to hold it up like a trophy for all the world to see: My trophy of womanhood — the guys that liked me. Then again, maybe some of them didn't really like me, and I just imagined they did...

I have to stop talking about guys liking me. I have to stop holding up that trophy, I thought. I had friends back home who did the same thing, and it drove me crazy. Yet here I was joining right in without ever realizing it!

And then there was Karl. Yes, I did think he liked me. *But did I like him?* It was just...he was too short. He had red hair. He wasn't my type.

It was the first time I saw what I was doing. The first time I realized my own hypocrisy, as I criticized guys for having too-high standards for a girl's physical appearance, and yet I held the same standards for guys. I berated guys for expecting too much from girls, expecting them to look like models, expecting them to be thin enough. Yet I walked right past guy after guy as though they were invisible, never seeing beneath the surface, looking only for height, brown hair, and milk chocolate eyes.

I thought I'd learned my lesson. I'd torn up that three-page list I carried back in the day, the list that perfectly described Eric. I realized that playing guitar, being in ministry, and even reading the Bible for an hour a day really didn't tell me anything about the guy's character. Integrity could only be played out in everyday life, watching the way he treated others, observing the way he received correction, enjoying everyday moments together, and seeing how he responded under pressure and in moments of temptation.

But I still found myself stuck on the cuteness factor.

Obviously I couldn't marry someone I *wasn't* attracted to! I mean, *c'mon*, I want to enjoy some fabulous sex with my husband someday!! And if I'm not even *tempted* by the person, I can't imagine actually enjoying getting *in bed* with him on our wedding night!

...But maybe I *could* be attracted to someone like Karl. Not because of my first glance, but because I saw deep into his soul and loved everything within him. Perhaps physical attraction could be diminished or enhanced by the core of a person — his personality, passion, humor, and character. Maybe attraction had to do with knowing a person, falling in love with the things that matter and will remain long after his skin wrinkles and sags. Looking back, even though Karl may have been the least attractive guy I'd been interested in so far (physically speaking), he was the most attractive to me. Perhaps attraction actually had little to do with first sight, and everything to do with looking a little deeper.

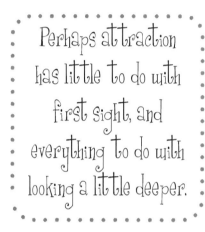

Perhaps attraction has little to do with first sight, and everything to do with looking a little deeper.

— love at last sight —

"I've got this hamburger with me for an object lesson," Dan, the assistant pastor at young adults, held up a one-pound burger, soaked through with grease. Eighty young adults groaned in disgust.

"And here's what I think. Sitting among you is a friend who eats more than anyone I've ever met. But I don't think even she can eat this whole thing."

I gulped, sensing what was coming. Part of me hated these food dares because of how guilty I felt afterwards, how much I wanted to starve myself the next day. But part of me just couldn't turn down a food dare! Couldn't resist the look of admiration on all the guys' faces. Couldn't say no to food. It was yet another form of disordered eating, another way food had become all or nothing to me. Another way this part of my life had swung out of control. Another way I was aching for guys' attention.

"Tiffany," Dan swiveled to face me. "I dare you to eat this whole burger after my object lesson."

My hand shot into the air. "Give it here! I will SO eat it."

Groans, laughter, a few cheers from the other young adults around me.

"Are you seriously going to do it?" a friend's face twisted in horror. "That's disgusting!"

Jenna laughed, "Oh, she'll do it alright! Just watch."

Karl was grinning wickedly as he got up to preach. A little knot had formed in my stomach, partly excitement and partly fear of that one-pound burger waiting for me. And then, there in the middle-of-nowhere Australia, everything changed.

I had heard Karl preach many times over the past three months, but tonight something struck me differently. Maybe the way he'd looked over at me before he started. Maybe the way his words struck an intoxicating mixture of passion and wisdom. Whatever happened, tingles ran up my spine. I felt like a window to his soul had opened, and instead of seeing red hair, I was seeing inside him. And everything I saw within him, I wanted.

Memories danced through my mind: exploring the Japanese Gardens under the stars, laughing long into the night, like old friends — rolling toilet paper down a hill to see how many squares high the hill was, the intensity of his gaze as he listened to my dreams, and the way his encouragement had made my heart come to life.

This was the kind of man I wanted to spend my life with. Someone pursuing the Lord with all his heart; someone with whom everyday moments became something special; someone who was chasing his life vision; someone who spoke life into others, prayed for others, encouraged others.

Maybe love at first sight was a myth. Perhaps it could turn into love, but it had to be tested first. With that I knew:

This was the night I fell for Karl, and it came when I looked a little deeper.

Dan's voice broke into my thoughts, as I watched Karl lope off the stage. "And now I do bestow this burger upon Tiffany," Dan announced. A grin broke out on my face as I walked up to the stage to retrieve my prize. "Let's see if you can eat it all."

"You betcha I can!"

(In case you're wondering, yes, I did eat the whole thing along with the fries. Then Karl said, "Bet you can't eat dessert too." So I did. Double-thick extra large milkshake. And *man* did I have a stomach ache afterwards!)

> Maybe love at first sight was a myth. Perhaps it could turn into love, but it had to be tested first.

— message in a Jenna —

Did he like me? I was dying to know. I mean, it used to seem so obvious, but now that I liked him, I just couldn't tell! Why hadn't he said anything yet?

One evening Jenna sauntered into my room grinning like a Cheshire cat.

"What's going on?" my eyes narrowed.

"I asked Karl if he likes you," her smile got bigger, as if that was possible, "*and he does.*"

"*What?!*" I shrieked, falling over the chair to reach her. Grabbing her arms I begged, "What did he say? What did he say?"

"Ohh...I don't know," she teased.

"Ahhh, tell me!!" I groaned in pure agony.

She laughed. "He says that you're exactly the kind of girl he's looking for, but he knows you're leaving so he doesn't want to let himself fall for you. He doesn't think it could work since you'll be gone soon. But if you were to stay here, I'm pretty sure he'd ask you out."

I squealed. "So he DOES like me!"

"Yeah, he does. He won't do anything about it, but he likes you." She paused, thoughtfully. "Oh wait, I told him I wouldn't tell you. Guess I forgot. Don't tell him I told." With that, she skipped down the hall.

— Swamp Foot —

The sunlight was so bright, the heat of spring hotter than a New York summer, when Jenna, Mike, Karl, and I decided to swing by the town reservoir. The state of Queensland was in an awful drought, so the water levels had dropped to ten percent of capacity. As we explored the reservoir, Karl teased me into chasing him. As I did so, I caught my foot in a swampy area, nearly losing my leg. Okay, that's a bit dramatic. In the end, I only lost my shoe and slathered my leg in mud.

"Swamp Foot! Get away from Swamp Foot!" Mike yelled in his Aussie accent, as he raced ahead to the car. Jenna and Karl rushed toward the front passenger seat.

"I don't want to sit next to her; she smells!" Karl said, grabbing the door handle.

"But I'm not sitting near the Swamp Foot; that's disgusting! You can, you're a guy!" Jenna batted him away.

"Let's just leave without her, guys!" Mike suggested.

I caught up, out of breath. "Don't you dare leave me here!" I pretended to be offended, but really, for the first time in my life, I was okay with the teasing.

I was okay with being muddy and smelly and imperfect.

I was okay having these crazy, sometimes intimidating, dreams for my life.

I was okay being smart and a little bit nerdy.

I was okay being me, even with guys around.

In the end, Karl slid in next to me, held his nose, and crammed as far away from me as he could get. I just moved closer to him. Man, I never wanted to leave this place, this moment. Could I hold onto this forever? I knew now that these friends loved me, not despite my quirkiness, *but because of it*. Because they'd looked a little deeper into me, too.

— Seasons —

The week before I left Australia, there was an urgency with which I approached each day, each moment, trying to soak it up like a person who would go without food and water for months, trying to take it all in before it was gone.

Richelle and I met for our final weekly "walk date." She'd become a dear friend over the past few months, as we met every other week for a lovely, inspiring talk while walking around town. When we started four months ago, frost had nipped at our breath. Now we had to meet early in the morning to avoid overwhelming heat.

This morning felt somber. In four days I'd be gone. This was the end, and I wished I could stop time like unplugging a clock.

"How do you feel about leaving?" she asked.

I almost couldn't speak for a second, as dread ate me up inside. "I don't want to leave. There's so much undiscovered potential! Like with Karl. There could be so much more, and yet here I am just walking away. It feels so stupid."

She nodded. She too had been there, had wanted to hold back seasons from changing.

"Actually, want to hear a song I wrote last night?" My eyes lit up as we passed the college music building.

"You wrote a song about it?! *Of course* I want to hear!" she squealed.

We ventured into the coolness of deserted practice rooms and found a baby grand piano. As I reached the chorus, tears filled my voice:

I know that I'll see you again
I feel it in my heart
But what will become of us now
the us we never had time to start
You're everything I've prayed for
on my knees as a little girl
And now in five days I'll be on
the other side of the world

When I finished, I looked over to see Richelle's eyes glistening. "Are you going to play it for him?" she asked softly.

Shaking my head, I knew the answer. *No. Not unless I saw him again someday.*

Suddenly that whole "getting as far away as you can" thing seemed less attractive. In just a few days, I would be gone. What then? It was like I'd come face to face with destiny just before time ran out and things went black.

Richelle waited a moment and then whispered, "Tiff, remember that you can't hold life's seasons back; you can't stop them from changing, or it'll stunt your growth. You have to keep walking into the next season."

"Wow, I've never thought of it like that." My hands stroked the keys in silence. "How many times I've tried to hold back one season or rush into a new one before its time. Especially with singleness. I've wanted to race out of this season, make it a short winter and early spring."

She nodded, "It's especially hard when friends are living in a different season than you."

"Yeah! It feels like they've all moved ahead of you, while you're stuck in winter. I've wondered sometimes if God has forgotten about me."

> You can't hold back life's seasons; you can't stop them from changing, or it'll stunt your growth.

"But He hasn't," Richelle clasped her hands around her knees as she continued. "And I've found that if I don't live each season to the fullest, I'll look back with regret. I won't learn everything I need to learn. If I bear fruit prematurely, it won't last the way it's meant to last."

I nodded. "And I want my future relationship to be almost effortless, something only God could do; something clearly covered by His fingerprints." I sighed, "Whether that's with Karl or someone else, the only way the relationship can be all it's meant to be is by living in the season He's given me. Not the season He's given *someone else*, but the season He's given *me*."

Maybe that's the only way to keep from becoming bitter too, I thought. With all eleven weddings I'd be attending next year, it would be easy to get angry and jealous. But if I remember to live in my own season and rejoice for others in their seasons, then maybe I won't get bitter.

After all, what is the goal of each season in life? Is it to be married? To be known and pursued and chosen? Is it to be doing amazing things for God? Is it to fulfill all the dreams in our hearts? Or is it something entirely different? Because maybe the goal of all seasons is one and the same, whether single or married, rich or poor, hidden in darkness or seen in the light: To love the Lord with all our heart and love other people as our self. Maybe I could live with joy in this season simply because I knew the journey's end was the same for all seasons. They all were designed to bring me to the same place: *Closer to Him.*

> The journey's end is the same for all seasons. They are all designed to bring us closer to Him.

I picked up a discarded pen from the piano bench and scribbled a bridge for Karl's song onto the paper in my pocket:

I know the right answers
But they don't make this any easier
How can I just walk away
Am I crazy just to wait
But I can't stop the seasons from changing
And you are not mine to hold onto

Richelle was right: he was not mine to hold onto. This season had somehow managed to slip through my fingers, even as I knew that was how it had to be.

— final snapshot —

Green suitcase looking on, Karl waited in line with me, chatting (in Japanese) with exchange students behind us. My heart could have burst.

Mike and Karl had driven Jenna and me to the airport. Mike had been teasing about Karl and I missing each other, but neither of us 'fessed up. We'd reminisced, shared our favorite memories, our favorite things about each other. Now Mike and Jenna were standing off to the side with two other dear, sweet friends from the church, who'd driven an hour and a half to see us off.

Karl and I didn't say much, just shuffled forward toward the baggage counter.

"Suitcase please."

Karl hefted my luggage onto the scale.

"And yours, sir?" The attendant's innocent question tore into my heart.

"Oh, it's just her today," he waved his hand like it was nothing, but we both knew it was everything.

What would have happened if I'd stayed? What would we have become? I pushed away the thoughts and absorbed the present reality, taking two seconds to package every one.

Mine was the first flight to leave. I hugged everyone for minutes on end, laughing shaky laughs at memories and jokes. Stepping through the gate, I left my heart behind. As the escalator carried me away against my will, I turned to wave, to say goodbye to the land I'd grown to love.

"See you State-side!" Jenna called, feigning cheerfulness. But I saw her chin trembling.

I grabbed a cup of coffee downstairs, and in my fumbling, shaky process, spilled a whole stack of napkins. As I bent to pick them up, a couple tears spilled over. I heard hooting from above and glanced up to see Karl, Mike, and Jenna leaning over the balcony railing, dying with laughter. I smiled through the tears.

Mike got down on one knee and yelled, "Tiffany, marry me!"

Karl's jaw dropped as he shouted back, "You can't do that!"

It's the last snapshot I have of Karl, one that's come back to taunt me many times. One that, for a long time, I wished I could erase with a new picture.

— not missing anything —

As time dragged its healing feet ever onwards, I graduated with my bachelor's degree, got a job back in Albany, NY, and home began to feel like home again, even as Karl began dating the woman who would become his wife a year later.

I often found myself wondering, *If I'd been prettier, would Karl have moved on? Would he have come to America and whisked me away with him? What did this new girl have that I didn't?* Once again the haunting feeling came: *I'm not the kind of girl that guys fall in love with. I'm not the kind of girl that gives them a reason to stay.*

Looking back, I understand that God had something else for me. I wasn't supposed to live overseas with Karl; He had something for me to do here in America. I also see the ways in which our lives intersected, but weren't heading the same direction long-term. And yet, he was the first guy with whom I'd so easily let down my act: the first one who encouraged me so sincerely in my dreams. And because of him, places of my heart came alive — places I'd nearly forgotten existed. And that made it hard to forget *him*.

"Someday he'll see what he missed out on!" my former roommate Krysta would tell me. I loved hearing those words; they made me feel relieved that maybe there was nothing wrong with me.

But one day I quietly considered their meaning, and came to a new conclusion. "Actually, I don't think he's missing out on anything."

"What?" Krysta looked like I'd gone crazy.

"I mean, it has nothing to do with how great I am, or how great he is. If we weren't right for each other, then no one's missing out on anything." I could hardly believe my ears. *Did I just say that??*

In fact, my mind finished, *the only way we'd be missing out on something is if we'd stayed together. Then we would have missed God's best for each of us.*

I was just beginning to learn that rejection was simply God's direction. It didn't mean there was something *wrong* with me; it meant He had something *else* for me. The hard part was trusting Him before I saw what that "something else" was.

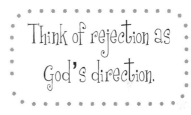

Think of rejection as God's direction.

BOY TALK

HOW TO LOOK A LITTLE DEEPER

Looking a little deeper was a huge step for me. One small step for woman, one giant leap for Tiffany — that kind of thing. Falling for Karl based on who he was, rather than what he looked like, was proof of a deeper work God was doing in my heart. These are some things I learned about looking a little deeper:

What I used to look for in a relationship: Someone with a charismatic and outgoing personality. Someone with specific talents (preaching, writing, and music). Someone who was going places in life, so much so that *everyone* noticed (which often played out as the guy bragging about everything he was doing). Someone that gave me status in our group of friends (hence why I was particularly drawn to people in ministry). Someone who looked a very specific way (certain height, hair, and eye color). Turns out, none of those things matter in life. *None at all.* Those things don't make a good husband. They don't give chemistry to a relationship. They are all outward things that would make me feel like I was awesome for getting the guy's attention, but that kind of "high" doesn't last long-term. It makes you feel good for a moment, but won't help a marriage one bit. In fact, those things could make a marriage much harder. Sometimes I've been way too particular about things that don't matter.

What I liked about Karl: His friendship. The way he encouraged me in my dreams and inspired me to be all God made me to be. His humor and adventurous spirit. My aunt once told me that if I don't enjoy everyday moments spent with a guy, I shouldn't marry him. She said you need to be with someone who makes the everyday moments seem special. Karl and I never fully developed this since we ran out of time, but we did have a lot of fun together, which was very important to me.

What I now look for: I've thrown out my old list of requirements for a future husband. (Good thing too, because no human being could *ever* fit all of them!) Instead there are just a few things I look for in a guy, and to be honest, I don't even have these written down; they're just a vague outline in my head. He needs to love God, love people, be hardworking, willing to learn, fun to be around, and have integrity (meaning, when no one is watching and he could get away with anything, he will still choose to be honest and trustworthy). And, of course, I need to be attracted to him. But that doesn't mean he has to be the most handsome man in the room; it just means we need to click in such a way that I find him incredibly attractive.

One other note: I always thought I needed a perfect prince charming, but such a person *does not exist*. No human is perfect. What I really need is a trustworthy man willing to grow, not a perfect man who has already arrived.

> What I really needed was a trustworthy man willing to grow, not a perfect man who had already arrived.

Looking back, I realize now that I still had a long way to go. A big part of my interest in Karl was because of his work in ministry. My mom told me I was falling in love with what a guy did, rather than who a guy was. I couldn't understand that concept at the time, but now I know it was true. Nevertheless, this season with Karl was the first step toward truly loving someone just because of who they were as a person.

DISCUSSION QUESTIONS

Use these questions as part of a small group, with a mentor, or on your own. As you prayerfully reflect on these, feel free to journal your thoughts in the spaces below each question.

1) Do you have a list of things you'd like in a future relationship? If so, what's on your list? Is there anything you would change to help yourself "look a little deeper"?

_____

_____

_____

_____

2) In learning to be myself, I realized my friends loved me not despite my quirkiness, but because of it, because my friends looked a little deeper into me. Do you have friends who see past surface things, and notice who you are as a person? If so, how did you develop those relationships? If not, how do you think you could develop those friendships? On a similar note, how can you look deeper into your friends?

_____

_____

_____

3) How can you live in the season you've been given? And how do you know what season you've been given?

_____

_____

_____

_____

4) How does this idea of rejection being God's direction impact the way you see relationships? How can you trust God before seeing the "something else" He has for you?

_____

_____

_____

_____

5 THE DREAMING YEARS

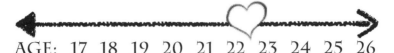

AGE: 17 18 19 20 21 22 23 24 25 26

Graduating college was weird. It was lonely moving back to Rochester, NY after my time in Australia and a semester at home in Albany. I thought living in Rochester would be just like college, but friendships had changed post-graduation, people had moved, and it felt like I was starting all over again. As much as I loved a new adventure, I hated starting over. It seemed to take years for me to find new, meaningful friendships.

I loved my first real job though; it was invigorating and rewarding to work in Residential Life at a college! I loved when students plopped down in my office and shared their hearts with me. There simply was nothing like it. But after work and evening graduate classes, what was there to do? You could only go grocery shopping so many times in a week. You could only clean so thoroughly. And then what?

When new acquaintances asked if there was a guy in my life, I shrugged noncommittally and said, "Oh, you know. Not right now. I'm too busy."

How I ached to say, "Yes! Want me to tell you all about him? He's wonderful and amazing, and I am now spoken for!" But instead I made excuses, explaining why I didn't really want the relationship my heart craved. I acted like it was no big deal, but then would spend lots of time on the phone with Austin, wishing he would see something in me worth fighting for.

— beautiful desires —

I had learned over the past few years that contentment doesn't take away desire; it surrenders desire. Because of that new understanding, there was a constant tug-of-war happening in my heart, a constant tension between surrendering and accepting the God-given desire for marriage.

> Contentment doesn't take away desire; it surrenders desire.

For years I felt guilt-ridden because I wanted to get married. I thought the desire meant I wasn't content, wasn't fully satisfied in Christ. But actually, the desire wasn't wrong. In fact, God planted that desire inside me and made it beautiful. It became even more beautiful when I surrendered it over and over, even while desperately wanting it.[19]

The hardest part was when well-meaning married friends told me, "You're so lucky to be single. Look at all the things you can do! Marriage is hard, but you have time to pursue your career and your dreams. I'm jealous of you." It would make me so mad! I just *didn't get it*. I'd think to myself, "If being single is *oh, so grand*, then why did you get married?! It's not like we live in the 1800s and you *have* to get married. You could have just broken up with the guy and stayed single forever!"

I knew they didn't really mean it when they said they were jealous. If that were true, people would pass up the

---

[19] *Some parts in this "Beautiful Desires" section were first edited by Rayni Peavy and released on her blog.*

love of a lifetime to be alone. But that's not normal. In real life, people get married even when they aren't crazy in love, just so they can have the companionship for life. Why? *Because we weren't made to be alone.*

And there the truth stood, staring me in the face day after day, night after night: *We were created for love.* In the beginning of the world, God made us for the kind of marriage companionship that I craved, embedding these desires into my DNA. When people encouraged me that being more satisfied in Jesus would take away my desire for a husband, I wanted to laugh. I thought about Adam in the Garden of Eden. It was just him and God, walking and talking together, but God still said it wasn't good for him to be alone. "If *that* was alone," I'd think, "then let me tell you – I'm *really* alone! At least Adam had God physically walking next to him! But who do I have?"

Some nights I woke up feeling like I was suffocating; I felt so alone that I was almost holding my breath without realizing it. Loneliness was a constant in my world. I'd pretty much given up trying to become happy about being single. I couldn't purge desire from my heart; all I could do was surrender it. It became all but a ritual: Every single day, sometimes every hour of the day, my heart fell to its knees and shared the words of Mary in Luke 1:38, "Let it be unto me according to Your word." *According to Your will.*

Sometimes the words came through angrily gritted teeth, other times they poured eagerly from my heart. "Not my will, but Yours. Always, Father. In *all* my life. There is no greater joy than to be in the center of Your will, so have Your way in my life, now and forever. I will follow wherever You lead."

In essence, surrendering my heart's desire said, "Lord, I want you even more than I want this dream." I was learning that He calls us not to despise our dreams, but to surrender them over and over, to wrestle with the desire, and to say, "I'm yours anyway. I choose you anyway."

I wondered why I had to be single, when there was nothing I was doing that required singleness. I wondered why I couldn't get married if I was just working a 9-5 desk job. But if there was anything I knew, it was that pain and brokenness were the only results of walking outside of His will and His time. It was only in surrender that I could find joy.

— home —

In those first weeks, months, and even two years of life back in Rochester, I often felt like I no longer had a home. I related more than ever before with verses about our calling as pilgrims and nomads, imagining that life on earth was just like studying abroad, waiting for our heavenly home.

One night, standing by my apartment window, I watched the gorgeous sunset as Hillsong's "Saviour King" played on repeat in the background. Remembering the last few weeks in Australia, I sang along, arms raised: "In Your freedom I will live!"[20]

That's when the realization hit me: *This is the smallest taste of what's still to come.* Perhaps the loneliness I'd felt throughout life was, in part, a perpetual ache for eternity, for the presence of God. I thought back on my newest favorite song by Brooke Fraser:

If I find in myself
Desires nothing in this world can satisfy
Then of course I'll conclude
That I — I was not made for here[21]

"Lord, please satisfy my soul," I prayed, pacing across my room. "I've longed for marriage, thinking that would satisfy my heart. Although relationships can probably help satisfy this longing for a little while, and although you've given me that desire, ultimately I'm realizing that this longing is for you and your presence. It's not so much a longing for marriage, although that is part of it. Instead this overwhelming loneliness is a longing for *you*. A longing for the home I was created for. A realization that I was not

---

[20] Hillsong. "Saviour King." <u>Savior King</u>. 2007.

[21] Brooke Fraser. "C.S. Lewis Song." <u>Albertine</u>. Wood & Bone, 2008.

made for here, and nothing here on earth can fully satisfy me."

Tears burned behind my eyes as I whispered, "God, you are my portion and the strength of my heart![22] Only you can satisfy."

— my story —

Teens thronged the hallways and lobbies as I dragged my keyboard behind me. "Excuse me, excuse me," I smiled, trying (as politely as possible) to push my way through the crowds, dodging vendor tables.

My first ever conference.

Over the last year, I'd shared my testimony with several different groups. First was the rehabilitation center in Costa Rica. While on a mission trip with Jenna, our team leaders found out I loved public speaking, and promptly asked me to share my story with the girls who had been rescued from sex trafficking and drug addiction. *What story?* I had thought, feeling overwhelmed with no idea what to say to these beautiful, broken young women. "Your struggles with beauty," the answer finally came in my prayer time the day before. I scribbled down my testimony, the struggles with disordered eating that I was still wrestling through, and shared it for the first time ever. The girls literally sat on the edge of their seats, tears pooling in their eyes as I spoke. Several pulled me and the translator aside afterward to share their own struggles. That night before falling asleep, I smiled up in awe at what God had done. I could barely believe what I had just seen: *how He had used my brokenness to bring life to others.*

After that trip, several other organizations asked me to share with small groups of women. I usually incorporated some of the songs I wrote on my journey; I always related better through music, and figured others might as well.

---

[22] *See Psalm 73:26.*

But this — this was the first big event I'd spoken at. There were close to two thousand teens swarming through this conference center! *What if my message wasn't totally accurate? What if no one wanted to hear what I had to say? What if I completely lost my train of thought and froze up?*

Never mind that I had spent nearly 100 hours preparing for this event. As I'd sat home alone, working away evening after evening, I'd thought into the emptiness, *At least this is one good thing about being single right now. I have uncontested time to pour into this.*

Mom had encouraged me to leave it in God's hands. "This won't be your best presentation ever, but it's okay not to be perfect. Each time you do this, the seminar will get better. It's okay to have a beginning."

"Excuse me," I called again, swerving around another table and nearly running over a teen racing through the maze.

Finally, in the quiet of one of the break out rooms, I drew a deep breath and set up my keyboard. *What if no one comes to my workshop?* I worried yet again. My sleep had been filled with nightmares of no one showing up for the event. Now *that* would be the worst rejection.

I needn't have worried. Twenty minutes before the scheduled start time, the room began filling. And filling. And filling. Soon there were no more seats. One of the ushers ran out to bring in more chairs. I had 250 girls packed into that meeting room, and this was only the first of my two sessions.

Trembling slightly, and yet beyond excited at the turnout, I stood to share my story, and something came alive inside me.

What moved me more than anything else was talking and praying with the girls afterwards. So many stayed behind to pray that I didn't have time to finish before the ushers cleared the room so the next packed session could begin.

I cried while sharing my story, I cried while praying with the girls. When I collapsed in the hotel room feeling like I'd run a marathon, I also felt alive — like I had never felt on a date or with a boyfriend. Alive like I had never pictured in my loveliest daydreams of marriage and love. *Something was changing.*

— star wars studio —

I stared at the battleground of Star Wars figurines staked out on his desk. Around the keyboard, amps, control panel — everywhere — the figurines thronged. Who *was* this guy?

I peeked at the business card my friend Mike had given me. Mike had toured with a band for several years, even appearing on MTV, and one night after I performed at our church talent show, he'd given me Brian's card. "If you ever want to record, my friend Brian is amazing," he'd said. So here I was.

I'd been looking for a recording company for about a year. After coming home from Australia, I'd tried three different places, but none of them left me crazy about the idea. Which led me to the Rochester, NY studio of this Star-Wars-infatuated producer.[23]

He caught me staring and offered, "I have a whole room full of my collection. Want to see it?"

"*There are more?*" I asked in disbelief.

I followed him across the studio and into a dark room. He flicked on the light and there before my eyes hung hundreds of collectibles still in their cases, perfectly lining the walls. My jaw dropped.

He laughed, "I've been collecting for a while. So let's hear these tunes you wrote! See if we can't work something out."

There is nothing like being in a recording studio to magnify a person's insecurities. I'd been slowly ending my love affair with the mirror and scale, but apparently my insecurities were deeper than just physical. Apparently at the core of my being, I never felt good enough.

Dejected, I opened the door of the recording room where Brian sat with my talented musician friends Nate and

---

[23] *Brian Moore's Red Booth Studio. See* www.redboothstudios.com.

Greg. *All of these guys are real musicians*, I thought. *I'm the faker.*

As Brian played back the scratch vocal recordings, preparing to lay Greg's drum tracks, I groaned.

"What's that?" Brian asked, pausing the music.

"All I can hear in these recordings are the mistakes! I hate it!" Granted they were just the scratch track, I hadn't even started recording the real takes...but I had no idea how out of tune my voice was! How awful it sounded!

Brian turned back to the computer, thinking. I almost thought he wasn't going to answer when he finally said, "But you know, both the mistakes and the good parts are equally important. Cause without the mistakes, we wouldn't have to be striving for this place of perfection. And if everything was perfect, it'd be boring."

I couldn't get those words out of my head all afternoon. Not for days, nor weeks afterward. I couldn't help thinking, *So if everything were perfect and right, we'd never know the pleasure of experiencing beauty, because we'd be accustomed to it. It's almost like without flaws you can't have beauty. Without a messed up world you can't know redemption. Without our weaknesses we can't appreciate God's strength. It's almost as if the flaws are just as integral for our understanding of what's good and right as the good and right parts are. If everything were perfect without our human mistakes, perfect would be meaningless.*

— Someday you'll thank me —

"Want to meet up in Syracuse?" Austin asked as I walked during my lunch break a few months later, phone clutched to my ear.

Syracuse was a half-way point along the four-hour drive from Albany (where he lived) to Rochester (home to yours truly). "Sure! When?"

"What about tomorrow? There's this really cool restaurant out there. I'll look up the name, can't remember off the top of my head, but they have peanuts everywhere.

You can just pick them up and eat them as you walk to your table."

I laughed. "Sounds great!"

Hanging up, I quickly dialed Nate and then Brian. "Hey! Would you mind if I sneak out of the studio early tomorrow while you guys are still recording?"

"What, because of a boy?" they both teased.

"Maybe."

The next day I got up an hour earlier than usual to make sure I looked as perfect as possible. I even had a new outfit to wear for the occasion! (*I know, I know,* the flaws are just as integral for our understanding of what's good and right...but I was still struggling with how that applied to my life, particularly to my body image.)

My little PT Cruiser could hardly contain all the nervous energy as I sped down the highway. *Will he think I'm cute?* I glanced in the rearview mirror, tilting it down toward me for the briefest second. *I feel really cute today.* After all these years, he knew me so well. Everything about me, in fact, except for one thing: *That I kept falling in love with him.* That I didn't miss Karl so much, because I had him. That I didn't date most of the guys who asked me out because I compared them to him.

We both ordered the same thing, including a side of sweet potatoes with marshmallows toasted on top. As the evening drew to a close, I found myself asking the one question I'd never dared ask before. "Austin, I know we're just friends, but why is that? Am I not pretty enough to date?"

His head shot up from the remains of his sweet potato. "What are you talking about, Tiff? Are you kidding? All my friends tell me I'm an idiot for not dating you!"

Exasperation overtook me. "Then why *don't* you date me?!"

He set aside his fork and looked me in the eye. "Tiff, I've thought and prayed about it many times, but every time I come away with this certainty that we're not supposed to be together."

He looked around, sighing. "Tiffany, you're on a very short list of girls I've ever met who have everything I'm looking for. You're very attractive, and when I met you, I wanted to date you, except I didn't realize you were so young and had a boyfriend. I mean, you were what, 17? And I was 23."

I snorted. "Yup, but that's *not* as big an age gap as you think it is!"

"Um, yeah it is. Maybe not as much now, but back at 17, that's a huge difference. It's like you came from a different culture!" He laughed. "Anyway. There have been many times I've thought about dating you, but every time, God has made it very clear to me that I am not the man He has for you. He has someone else for you. Someone who can love you like your dad loves your mom. I don't know how to do that."

I pictured my parents, the way they cared for each other, the way my dad treated my mom like a princess, the way I felt so beyond lucky to see that picture of what marriage was meant to be. Yes, I wanted that kind of relationship someday. Longed for it. But why couldn't I have that with him? I mean, when I imagined us together, that's how it looked — just like my parents' relationship. But then again…maybe that was the problem: *my imagination.* Always dreaming of how I wanted things to be, which clouded my judgment to see how things *really were.*

Looking down, he added, "If we dated, I know my weaknesses. I'd push things too far physically, and then if we broke up…well, I want to be able to go to your wedding, shake your husband's hand, look in his eyes, and tell him I always honored you." Tears pushed into my eyes as he sat back in his seat and finished, "My choice not to date you has nothing to do with you not being pretty enough or good enough. It's because I am convinced that God has someone else for you."

In all my life, I'd never felt more loved than I did at that moment. It gave a whole new meaning to the word. I felt more cherished and respected than I ever had by a guy I dated, more worthy than I ever had when a guy's eyes flitted across my body. I squeezed my eyes shut to hold in the soft tears, and smiled in spite of myself. "What if I disagree?"

"You can disagree, but I am 100% sure of this. Someday you'll thank me."

— Someday —

I sat hinged on the edge of my bed, guitar in hand, trying to work out the right words for my song "Someday." In the studio yesterday Nate had brought up an interesting point: "Tiffany, I love your song 'Someday.' I think it's going to be a hit. But in the bridge you say God's preparing the right prince, and I'm wondering if that's really what you want to say."

I thought back on the lyrics:

If you're a daughter of the King
Then you don't have to go on worrying
He is preparing the right prince
Who'll fit you perfectly
So someday you'll see
You'll walk down the aisle...

"The point of the song," I argued, "is to tell girls — and myself — that they don't have to worry about if they'll get married; God will take care of it. They'll get married someday."

"But is that really the point? Getting married, I mean. And does God really guarantee that?"

I hated that he asked that question, because I didn't want to ask it myself. What *was* the point? Was it getting married, or was it walking the path God has for us, believing that in His presence is fullness of joy,[24] believing that He can satisfy our hearts? That question challenged me to the core.

I thought back on when I had turned 21. In a moment of inspiration and freedom, I'd written in my journal, "If I have to wait until I'm 25 to get married, I'm okay with that!" I had been amazed at God's miraculous work that allowed me to write such a thing.

Now I was sitting here on my bed two years later. Still okay with waiting until age 25 for marriage, but unsure if I could wait another day past that.

---

[24] *See Psalm 16:11.*

I called my dad and asked him the question Nate asked me. Then I talked with friends. And now here I was planted on my bed with my garage-sale guitar, rewriting the bridge and chorus:

When you're a daughter of the King
Then you don't have to go on worrying
He is preparing the right path
That'll fit you perfectly
So someday you'll see

You'll walk down His aisle
With flowers in your hair
And sparkling glass slippers
Your very own pair
And someday you'll see — it's happening[25]

Yes. *His aisle.* His path. Wherever that aisle led, whether to a man waiting beside an altar or to an orphanage overseas or to a cross-country speaking adventure, it was the only aisle that could ever bring a person true joy.

— more is coming —

Voices of loudspeakers drowned into my peripheral, as did the scores of scurrying people and luggage. My friend Joanna and I sat off to the side of the airport terminal, waiting for our flight to Florida. A Christian college was flying us down so I could share my story at their chapel service, and then spend an extra day at the beach.

I couldn't believe it! I used to dream of speaking at colleges and conferences, and now a college was flying me down to do just that! *This is absolutely crazy!* I nearly giggled out loud. *These dreams are starting to come true!*

---

[25] Tiffany Dawn. "Someday." <u>This Is Who I Am</u>. 2011.

Though I was overjoyed to be sitting here beside Joanna, awaiting the beaches, part of me still wished I could share the flight with my husband. Write this story together. Dream and plan and speak side-by-side.

My mind drifted. When I was speaking I felt more alive than I ever felt on a date. Something sprang up inside me — this energy, this purpose — something I'd never known existed. Without calling or forcing it out, this energy came of its own accord.

I whispered a prayer into the crowded terminal. "Thank you for letting me come to life even in the waiting. Thank you for giving me something to do. Thank you for beginning to fulfill these dreams in my heart."

In that moment, facing floor-to-ceiling windows overlooking the runway, I felt something in the deepest part of my being: *More is coming.* I just knew it was.

— once more —

There was something missing from the album. After nearly a year of recording in the slowest possible manner for the sake of my wallet (record for three days, then take a two month break; record another three days, take a three month break; and so on), we had nearly finished the CD. And yet... *something.* Something wasn't there that needed to be there. Another song that hadn't been born yet.

As winter found its way to New York yet again, something else was missing too. I kept thinking back on the summer's conversation with Austin. Why hadn't I been fully honest? Why hadn't I told him exactly how I felt? Sure he knew I was interested, but did he know just how interested I was? I had to tell him. What if he married someone else, and I was left to forever regret my lack of honesty?

I traveled back to Albany for the holidays and planned to meet up with Austin while there. It hit me as I awoke that morning: *The day for courage had arrived.*

No sooner had we met at a coffee shop than he decided we should go Christmas shopping. Traversing store after store, I fought down butterflies in my stomach and hardly said a word the whole afternoon we spent together.

As day drew into evening and darkness settled around us, he headed back to drop me off at my car, where we'd met hours ago. I was out of time. I knew I couldn't put it off another minute.

"Austin, I have to be honest with you, or I'm afraid I'll regret it the rest of my life. Please don't let this be awkward."

"Okay," he maneuvered through pre-holiday traffic crowding the road.

"When I picture my life, it's with you standing beside me. You're the person I want to spend my life with. I think we could be really good together. And…yeah. I just have to tell you that."

I watched his face nervously. A smile spread across his lips. "I've been thinking the same thing." He switched on his blinker to turn left.

"Really?" I went numb all over for sheer joy!

"Yeah. I've been praying about us a lot again, and I, too, think we could be really good together. But, Tiff, if we got married, I would be getting a great deal. You'd make an incredible wife. But you wouldn't be getting such a great deal. I wouldn't be the kind of husband you deserve."

"Would you let *me* be the judge of that?" I shot back.

"Sure, you can be the judge of it, but I couldn't live with myself if I did that to you. The only reason you like me is because you don't know enough good guys."

"That is NOT true!"

"Yes it is. So, let's do this. You go and date different guys for a few months — join an online dating service or whatever, just get to know different guys, good guys. If you still like me afterward, then I'll talk with you about going on a date."

"That's so stupid. It's not going to change anything," I crossed my arms defiantly as we pulled into the parking lot.

"I think it will," he replied gently. "I think it'll change everything."

— love Song —

Everyone else was also out Christmas shopping when I got back to my parents' house. Wandering upstairs, I left the lights off in my room, replaying our conversation. I'd done all I could; now he knew, and hope surged through me. Maybe after three months we could actually date!

In the dim lighting, I picked up my guitar, emotions coursing through me. Cradling the guitar cross-legged on my floor, I wrote the most beautiful song I'd ever dreamed: *all for him.*

> *I've had my doubts, I've had my reasonings*
> *Explanations why this wasn't meant to be*
> *But now I see*
> *Honesty has not been found in my vocabulary*
> *I work up the courage just to watch it disappear*
> *But not this time, no not this time*

Finally I had found the courage for honesty. *Finally.* And now I felt again, deep in my being, that I wanted to share my life with him. The open acoustic chords morphed into what would become the chorus, perfectly expressing all the feelings only hinted at, the words left unsaid:

> *You are the one I want to be with*
> *Yours is the hand I want to hold*
> *I want to come home to you and sleep beside you*
> *Every single night*
> *With you I want to share my life*[26]

Even while writing it, I knew this is what was missing from my album. *This love song.* It was the missing puzzle piece. I could finish the CD now.

---

[26] Tiffany Dawn. "Giving In." <u>This Is Who I Am</u>. 2011.

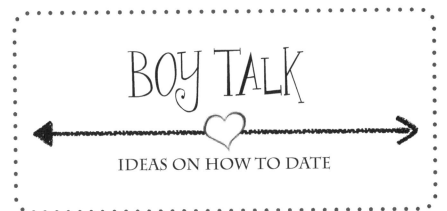

BOY TALK

IDEAS ON HOW TO DATE

Austin encouraged me to go on dates with different guys, and at the time I couldn't believe he would suggest such a thing! Well, guess what? I know this might sound weird, but I am now a huge proponent of casual dating, particularly after high school.

Through high school, I felt like the only one of my friends who had never dated or been asked out. There can be a lot of pressure to date during high school, to be a girl with a boyfriend, but I encourage you to focus on developing healthy, strong friendships with people of both genders instead. Not only can dating really hurt your heart, especially at that age, but it also takes up so much emotional and physical time and energy, that it can detract from the other friendships and activities you're involved in. Honestly, when you're in high school, the chances of you marrying anyone you date are extremely low. I do have friends who were high school sweethearts, but I also have friends who got into a relationship or stayed trapped in a relationship just for the sake of the story of being high school sweethearts. Instead, pursue your interests and build friendships, rather than giving everything up just for the sake of a boy. This section about casual dating is more specifically written for people who are in a season of life where they feel emotionally and spiritually ready to date.

Once you're in college or post-college, in my opinion and personal experience, going on dates with different guys helps us learn a ton about ourselves and about what we want and need in a future relationship. So here are some ideas that I'd encourage you to talk and pray about with trusted adults in your life, to see whether or not casual dating might be helpful for you too:

1) Date casually. I know I already said this, but I want to explain further. By "dating" in this context, I am not referring to boyfriend-girlfriend relationships, although I absolutely think those relationships can also be helpful when done safely and wisely. What I mean by "dating" in this context is going out on dates with lots of different trustworthy guys. This helps protect our hearts while learning about ourselves and others. Not getting physical, not thinking about marriage, not daydreaming about the guy; just a date. Like how our grandparents went to get soda and talk at the corner store. That kind of thing.

2) Date safely. Tell someone where you'll be on your dates and when to expect you home. If you don't know the guy really well, drive yourself (or have someone drop you off and pick you up), rather than riding with your date. You don't want to end up in a dangerous situation.

3) Date in groups as well as individually. Going out with a group of friends is a great way to get to know people! (If you're a teenager and would like to date, this is a particularly good way to do it.) There's no better way to get to know someone than to see how he interacts in a group setting (or with his family!), not just when he's putting his best foot forward with you.

4) Learn how to talk about different topics. Here's what I mean. I've gone on dates with some people who can only talk about one or two topics. Outside of those things, they have nothing to say! One guy in particular only knew how to talk about cars. Anything else, *silence. Man*, was that a long date, and I couldn't wait for it to end! It made me realize that I should learn how to talk about a wide variety of topics. I don't have to be an expert in them, but if I can carry on a conversation about a variety of things, not only will the date flow more smoothly, but it will also help me learn about the other person and their interests. Being able to talk with people is an excellent skill for all areas of life, from work to friendships to ministry. If you struggle to talk about certain topics, do some research or even read one of the many books that are now published about how to start conversations with anyone. If you get nervous, just do what a mentor once told me: Focus on making the other person feel comfortable, and then you'll stop noticing how nervous you feel. Let me tell you, *it really works!*

5) Practice being approachable. Sometimes our facial expressions and mannerisms give us an air of being stand-off-ish or uninterested, when really we're just afraid or stressed. Look in the mirror at your normal face, and see how it might be read by people who don't know you. Be aware of that baseline when you are interacting with other people, whether those you just met, friends, or a date. Practice smiling more often, giving sincere compliments, making small talk with random people you meet, and laughing. This will not only help while on a date, but will also help you *meet* dates!

6) If you get in a relationship, make sure you both like each other! I've run after so many guys who really weren't interested in me. Honestly, it was simply because of my pride; I felt like a failure if I couldn't win over any guy I wanted to, so I chased guys who didn't have interest. Even with Austin, I should I have realized that he wasn't super into the idea of dating me, and let go of my daydreams of being with him as more than a friend. It's hard to do that, but in the long run, why waste your time with a guy who doesn't really want to be with you? I'd rather be in a real relationship where we both care about each other equally.

7) Have fun! This is probably the most important part of all these tips. Take the pressure off, because this date doesn't have to lead to anything more. Relax and enjoy getting to know yourself and someone else better!

8) Remember: This is just a date. Just because you go out with a guy once, you don't have to go out again. Take it one date at a time. If someone asks you out for coffee, drink coffee with him. You don't have to figure out if he's your husband after your first coffee. Try to live in the present, and don't let your mind run wild, making up an idea of who this person might be. Instead, get to know who they are.

In closing, let me clarify that I don't go on dates with just anyone. For example, if I don't want to go on a date with someone, or if I get a weird vibe, then I don't go. That's totally fine. However, if a guy asks me out who seems interesting and trustworthy, I'll usually go on a date with him, even if he's not my "normal type" physically speaking. Actually getting into a boyfriend-girlfriend relationship is another story entirely. In that case, I only have boyfriends I think have marriage potential, because I don't want to give my heart away just for the sake of not being alone. But casual dating? Well that's a great way to get to know myself and others. It's also a great way to get to know men who are different than the kind of guys I'd usually spend time dreaming about.

DISCUSSION QUESTIONS

Use these questions as part of a small group, with a mentor, or on your own. As you prayerfully reflect on these, feel free to journal your thoughts in the spaces below each question.

1) What is your perspective on singleness? What things help you enjoy life right where you are, whether in a relationship or single?

_____

_____

_____

_____

2) What do you think about that hard question Nate asked: "Is marriage really the goal? Does God guarantee it?" How do you feel about that?

_____

_____

_____

_____

3) I've found that the loneliness I feel may be a longing for the presence of God, more than anything else. What do you think about that? Do you feel lonely? What helps fill that loneliness?

_____

_____

_____

_____

4) Have you ever felt that constant tension between surrendering and accepting your God-given desires? What does that tension and process of surrender look like for you?

_____

_____

_____

_____

5) What do you think about "casual dating?"

_____

_____

_____

_____

6 THE TRAVIS YEARS

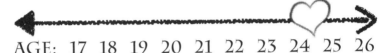

AGE: 17 18 19 20 21 22 23 24 25 26

Springtime bloomed around me as I pulled into my parking spot one night. The stillness of the atmosphere reflected in my heart. Not only were my three months drawing to an anticlimactic close — the three months before Austin would consider dating me — but I also hadn't kept my end of the bargain (dating different guys, like he'd said I should). In fact, I hadn't dated *anyone at all.*

That afternoon, a man I once thought could be "the one" (I didn't really know him at all; basically he was just cute and in ministry), had appeared out of nowhere and introduced me to his beautiful, composed fiancé. My heart had the wind knocked out of it. Now, at 10:00PM, it was still struggling to catch its breath.

Locks ground open on my apartment door, and I flipped on the light to reveal the emptiness I felt. An empty kitchen. Empty bed. Empty living room. *Always empty.* Always exactly how I'd left it that morning.

I kept my life busy; it helped me feel happier: Building rich friendships. Pursuing my dreams. Getting my master's degree. Paying off loans. Leading Bible studies. Mentoring others. Serving at my church. Having an outlet for my energy and passion made me much, much happier. And yet, on days like today, it didn't matter how many people I saw or how late I stayed out; as soon as I walked back into my lifeless apartment, I wanted to dissolve into the emptiness.

Although it was a work night, the intensity of tonight's feelings drowned out my ability to sleep. I tried writing and reading, but I couldn't focus. Finally I picked up my phone and texted several friends, asking if anyone was free to meet up. The only one who responded with a "yes" was Travis.

I typed, "Never mind, no one else is free so I guess we won't do anything tonight," and then paused. Normally I wouldn't think twice before coffee with a friend, but recently I'd found myself wondering if he wanted more than friendship, which is why I paused. And yet...I was so lonely. *I need to be around someone right now — anyone!* I thought. *I don't want to lead him on, but really...I'm desperate. He'll understand.*

I erased the text and rewrote, "See you at the late-night Coldstone in an hour!" That ice cream shop was the only place open so late on a Sunday night.

— Superman —

I'd met Travis a few years prior. He had (quite literally) super-manned into my life. The only thing missing from that moment was the theme music.

My friend Ashley had invited me to a Bible study, saying, "Tiffany, there's this super cute, sweet, godly guy at my Bible study...and he's *single*!! My husband Levi even likes him. We want you to meet him!" So I went.

It was one of my more daring moments. I guess I was one of those girls who thought a guy would show up on her doorstep one morning, wrapped in sparkly pink packaging with the note: "To Tiffany, From God: Contains 'The One.'" In more recent years I decided that approach was a bit weird and stalker-ish, so if I wanted to meet a good guy, I'd better go where the good guys were.

When a friend asked in disbelief why I'd gone to a Bible study to meet a guy, I had to laugh. I understood her concern, but thought, *I don't get it! There's nothing else in life that we just wait around for. We apply for jobs and colleges; we go to small groups for the purpose of making friends; we "try" with our husbands to have babies. It's the biblical principle of sowing and reaping. So why is finding a husband any different — and what better place than a church event to find a guy who is serious about God?*

In fact, in biblical times, people went out specifically *looking* for a spouse. Abraham sent his servant, told him exactly where to go and what to say, to find a wife for his son.[27] So wouldn't it be okay for us to go where good guys are, to position ourselves in places where we can meet godly men?

And maybe it was okay to be approachable too. After college, I started training myself to be cold toward guys, partly so I wouldn't lead guys on by flirting, and partly so no one could tell if I liked a guy, so they'd never know if he didn't like me back. (I'm sensing a theme in my life called "fear of rejection.") My sister told me it was rather arrogant to assume guys were going to like me, and therefore act coldly toward all of them from the day I met them. I didn't like hearing that, but realized it was true. I had to re-train myself to be approachable, treating everyone with kindness and in a friendly manner. That meant, smile and be interested in other people's lives.

Each year that passes, I'm more convinced that it's okay to put ourselves out there and show our interest in guys that we like. Sure, we can be too much of a flirt, but we can also be too afraid of showing interest. I feel like someone needs to say this, for the sake of girls like me who have felt guilty for wanting guys' attention. So I'll say it: *It's okay to go on a date. It's okay to get coffee with a guy you haven't quite figured out whether or not you like. It's okay to smile and make small talk with a cute guy. It's okay.*

And I'll get off my soap box now.

All of that to say, I assured my friend that I had another Bible study I attended regularly, as well as a church family and mentors. But, the group that night? Well, I was

---

[27] *See Genesis 24.*

honest with myself and others. *The only* reason I went was to meet this guy Ashley was raving about.

The girls were already comfy in high top chairs with warm coffee when Travis tripped through the door. He blinked at us and then proceeded to fling himself down the stairs toward the guys' group.

Literally fling himself!

He never told me if he accidentally fell or purposefully threw himself down the stairs. Either way, he gracefully caught himself in a somersault the same moment he caught my attention. Right then and there I decided we were long-lost twins. But *just twins*, just friends.

I don't know about you, but I have this thing I call "instant judgment," where I immediately decide that I know who a guy is and how I feel about him, even though I have no idea who he is. (Usually my instant judgment is based solely on his cuteness level and ministry involvement, although I never admit that at the time.) In this case, I instantly thought I didn't like Superman in the dating kind of way, but I definitely wanted to be his friend.

That was two years ago, and now here I was in an unexpected situation: sitting across from him in a last-minute meet-up. I wasn't normally one to give guys a chance; I would simply think to myself, *Do I want to be with this guy? Nah, I don't think it's right*, and therefore would never get to know him. (As if I could know if I liked a guy without ever talking to him!) I acted like coffee meant I had to date or (*gasp*) marry the guy, so I'd better avoid it at all costs! Yet here I was across from Travis, wondering why two years ago I'd so quickly decided I didn't want to date him. Wondering why I'd waited so long to get coffee (or ice cream) with him. Wondering if maybe I should be more open to giving trustworthy guys a chance when they had the courage to ask me out.

I talked, ice cream melted, and he listened. *Really* listened, the way few know how to do, asking the right questions, saying the right amount. As the clock ticked onward, I glanced at my phone. 2:00AM?? I *never* stayed up this late on a work night! *Ever!* "Oh my gosh, I have to run!" I shoved the phone into my bag and began collecting our trash. "I'm so sorry I talked the whole time, but thank you so much for listening! This was really nice."

"Of course!" He held the door for me and walked me to my car.

I turned to give him a quick hug before slipping away, but he held on. He didn't let go for what seemed like ages. My rigid spine melted and I hugged him back for dear life.

Wow, I haven't been hugged in so long! I know I'm not a hugger, but especially being away from my family, there's been no one to hold me. How I've missed this! I think I've been quite literally starving for physical touch. And now that I've tasted it, how can I let go again?

When we finally parted, something had changed in me. *Accidentally.*

Maybe Austin was right, I thought, driving slowly home. *Maybe this will change everything.*

— the possibility —

I never talked with Austin after those three months ended. Partly because I hadn't dated, but also because I wasn't sure if he really wanted to date me. Sometimes I felt like his afterthought, like the good idea after the others were gone. If he really wanted to date me, wouldn't he have dated me a long time ago? But I didn't dwell on those thoughts. Anyway, here at the end of those three months, I had found a new side to Travis, a new side to the man who would make me wonder if maybe God did have someone else for me, someone other than Austin.

We were drinking coffee in their living room the first time I mentioned Travis to my mentors, the DuPrés.

Mrs. DuPré nearly shot out of her seat like a bullet from a canon. "We LOVE him!! Yes, yes, yes! You guys would make the cutest couple EVER!"

Laughing, Pastor Mark DuPré put his hand on her arm. "Honey, we don't want to scare her! You know how skittish she is about relationships." Then to me, "But we absolutely love Travis. He's a wonderful guy. One we trust." He paused, thinking. "So if you were my daughter, this would be my advice: Don't think too far ahead. Don't try to figure out if you're going to get married down the road. You tend to live in the future too much. Just take things slow, be in the moment, and enjoy getting to know one another. He's a trustworthy man."

I took a deep breath. How very different than the way I'd approached dating in the past! Growing up, I thought it was godly to immediately look ahead to marriage, but that only ended up tearing my heart apart with Eric. I took things too seriously, rushed to figure out if we should get married, and confused emotion with truth. Maybe if I'd taken things slower, simply gotten to know Eric, and waited to give my heart away, I would have seen the relationship from an unbiased perspective, and wouldn't have been hurt as deeply.

"Don't get physical either," Pastor Mark warned. "Take it slow in every respect. Spend time together with friends, get another couple to hold you accountable to staying pure (physically), and then simply enjoy. See what happens. Maybe he's right for you, maybe he's not, but you can't know that yet, because you don't know him."

"Okay," I nodded. "So if he asks me out, I'll say yes." Then panic struck. "But what if he doesn't bring it up? What if he doesn't like me?"

They threw back their heads and laughed together. "I'm sure he will bring it up," Pastor Mark chuckled. "As a matter of fact, I'm grabbing breakfast with him later this week. I bet he'll mention something then."

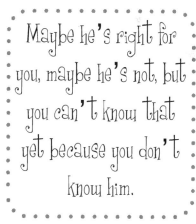

Maybe he's right for you, maybe he's not, but you can't know that yet because you don't know him.

"Would you tell me what he says?" I asked eagerly.
"No way! You'll have to wait and see."

— walking in circles —

My friend Joel and I were walking in circles around the block. Travis still hadn't arrived at the Fourth of July weekend picnic, and my nerves were ruining the party for me. Maybe he wouldn't come. At this point, that was a welcome possibility.

When we came around our loop for the third time and saw Travis looking for me, I pretended not to see him. "Let's go around again," I ducked away from the fence and tugged Joel after me.

"Tiff, you can't run forever! At some point you have to see him," he leaned toward me like an older brother, offering advice while laughing at my discomfort.

"I know, just one more time around. Only one more; I promise."

He gave me a knowing look as if to say, *Yeah right.* "I'll make *sure* it's only once more."

"It's just scary. Eric's the only guy I've ever officially dated, and I guess deep down...I still expect every other guy to treat me like he did," I explained for the hundredth time.

"I know."

"I mean, I like him, but now that he's shown too much interest, I want to run. I just can't do it. Joel, I feel like I'm going to throw up, I'm so scared!"

He laughed his raspy laugh. "Tiff, I know. We've been through this a hundred times. You've felt this way with every guy. You just have to push through it."

I shook my head. My heart had shut down without my permission; I couldn't pry it open again. I hid in my fear, preferring to be alone rather than risk my heart.

"You can do this, Tiff. He's a good guy, and I'll be here for you," Joel draped his arm around my shoulders, then teased, "Plus, I'm sick of hearing about it, so hurry up and date him already!"

We reached the end of our walk all too soon. "One more time around?" I asked, half-hoping he'd give in.

"Nope!" Joel swung open the gate to the picnic area and marched straight to Travis. "How's it going Travis? We were just talking about you!"

— cliff adventures —

"Looks like the sun is about to set." Travis reclined in his chair as the picnic wound down.

I scanned the sky and nodded. "Mmm."

"I know the perfect place to see the sunset. It's beautiful. Want to go?"

I glanced at Joel. It looked like he'd answer for me if I didn't. After the briefest hesitation, I agreed. "Let's do it."

I tailed Travis' sports car to a nearby beach. As we climbed out of our cars, sure enough the sky was turning all different shades of purple.

"This way," Travis pointed toward the woods.

"Are you sure? The beach is that way."

"No, there's a different spot this way that's really beautiful."

Brushing away cobwebs and ducking under tree branches we hiked a short distance into the forest before coming upon a sparkling clear opening, overlooking a high cliff with the lake below. When my mouth fell open at the view, Travis looked pleased.

"It might be easier to climb barefoot down the sand," Travis advised. "I can carry your shoes."

"Oh gosh, this is steep! I don't know if I can do it without falling!"

He grinned. "You'll be fine; I'll help you." Turning sideways he took our shoes in one hand and my hand in his other. "Just one step at a time; we'll be good."

I squealed as my feet slid forward on the sandy cliff. Digging in my heels and clutching his hand, I caught myself.

"I gotcha," he laughed.

"How are you doing this walking backwards? Are you sure you're good?"

"I'm okay, I want to make sure you get down safe."

His chivalry sent giggles down my spine. "Ooohh, look at the sky! This is beautiful!" I paused for a second in our descent. This truly would be a breathtaking sunset. Did he plan to ask me out tonight? Did I *want* him to ask me out?

As I stood looking up, I heard a muted thud. Glancing down, I saw our shoes tangled up in the sand and Travis on his knees. His right arm hung at an odd angle, his left hand pushing him back onto his feet. Within seconds his face had turned white as the sand and little beads of sweat squeezed out onto his forehead. Cradling his right arm, he managed, "I have to get out of here."

"Are you okay?"

His shoulder jutted out, as though it were misplaced. He couldn't answer, just nodded and somehow pushed quickly up the cliff and back through the woods, completely disappearing before I fully realized what had happened.

"Oh gosh," I thought, turning to follow him back up. Only — *I couldn't.* I looked up and down. Where to go? How to get out? It was too steep!

Panic crept into my throat. Travis was gone through the woods and my cell phone was in the car. Why was I so stupid?[28] What if I was stuck here forever? What if he passed out and I couldn't get help to him?

I climbed 12 inches up and promptly slid three feet down. Grasping for blades of grass and twigs jutting from the sand, I felt sweat breaking out on my forehead. Travis was probably passed out on the path, being eaten alive by wild animals. And meanwhile I'd die of thirst on this secluded stretch of beach!

What I really needed was a rescue team. Where were the Navy SEALS when you needed them? Who would know where to look for me?

---

[28] *Let me insert a comment here about bringing your cell phone on dates. You don't want to be stuck on a secluded beach, or worse! I also must note that I never would have gone to a secluded beach with Travis if I had just met him. After two years of friendship within a community of people who cared about me, I knew Travis was trustworthy. But if I didn't know and trust him, I never would have ventured out alone with him to this beach.*

At last I spotted another path, a few hundred yards to my right. Wobbling along the connecting stretch of sand halfway up the embankment brought me to the other path. Though slightly less steep, I still didn't think I could climb it. Staring it up and down, I tried to formulate a plan through my panicked thoughts.

The only possibility would be to propel myself up by sheer acceleration. I backed up a couple steps, willed my muscles to work, and took a running start up the cliff. I collapsed just at the edge and pulled myself the rest of the way, then darted back through the woods looking everywhere for Travis' body.

He was leaning against my car, barely conscious. I opened the hatchback and helped him sit down. "I'll drive you to the hospital, it's not far," I offered.

"No...no. I'm...about to pass...out. Don't want to... pass out...on you."

I tried arguing, but he wouldn't hear of it, so I called 911. The emergency vehicle couldn't arrive soon enough. They strapped Travis up and loaded him in.

I followed them to the hospital, talking to Joel on my Bluetooth as I drove. When I pulled up at the emergency entrance they asked, "Are you his girlfriend?"

What was I supposed to say? *Sort of? Maybe I would have been tonight if it wasn't for that stupid cliff?*

"N-nooo," I drew it out, unsure.

"Want me to come keep you company while you wait?" I heard Joel's voice asking over my Bluetooth.

"Yes! Please!" I sounded desperate.

He laughed, "Thought you'd need the company. I'll be right over."

As it turns out, Travis had slipped and fallen in such a way that he managed to dislocate his shoulder. The pain made him lightheaded for several hours until they were able to finish the x-rays and pop his shoulder back into place.

Joel and I talked in the waiting room, easing my nerves. Travis' mom met us there. She spent most of the time with her son, but came back to meet me and chat for a few minutes. Talk about awkward. *Hey, I'm the girl who made your son dislocate his shoulder 'cause he was carrying my shoes.*

— going steady —

A few days later, right arm in a sling, Travis sat beside me on the couch watching our favorite spy show. (That is, *my* favorite spy show. He enjoyed it mostly because I did.)

Munching on the snacks he'd brought for me, I turned toward him. "Why are you so nice to me?"

He smirked and shrugged with his good shoulder. "I don't know... Maybe I like you a little."

I grinned and turned away from him. A good minute passed, enough time to make him squirm, as I decided what to say. I couldn't come up with anything smart. "I might like you a little too."

His laugh was edgy. "That was quite the hesitation there."

"I know, just wanted to make you sweat." But really, deep down, I just wasn't sure. It didn't feel right. But how was I supposed to know? I *did* like him. Or maybe I *could* like him.

"Uh-huh," he didn't sound convinced.

"No, really. I do like you," I made my voice stronger.

"So...would you want to go out with me?"

"You mean, like, on a date? Or, like...I don't know... going steady or whatever they call it?" I beat myself up inside. *Going steady? Who says that?*

He grinned, "Would you go steady with me?"

A slow smile spread across my face. *Was this really happening?!* He was actually asking me out?! This didn't happen to me — ever! And then, in the next moment, fear churned in me. *What should I say? Could I do this? Could I actually date someone again?* I tried to stay in the moment as I nodded. "Yes. I would like that."

The next morning I didn't feel any differently. It wasn't like when Austin and I talked about dating. When we'd talked about dating I'd felt like I was floating away with bubbles. Instead, I felt happy and nervous. *That was it.* Honestly, I kind of wanted to say we were dating but never actually go on a date, that way I could know the joy of having a boyfriend without knowing the throwing-up sensation of actually investing in him. I know it sounds weird, but going out with someone, being *vulnerable* with someone, scared me so badly that I felt like I was going to throw up each time I saw Travis. As much as I wanted a boyfriend, it would have been kind of nice to not have to *see* him.

— how to know —

Shouldn't I know by now if he's the one? We've been talking for a few months and going on dates for a few weeks already! I was laying on my bed, thinking myself to sleep. Or, rather, thinking too much to fall asleep.

Shaking my head, I tried to shake away the doubt. In a culture of Disney movies and Josh Harris books, I'd dreamed of the day I'd meet my future husband. In an instant I would know he was the one, before we ever met for our first coffee; *I was sure of it.* So why didn't I feel that with Travis?

My mom said she never "knew" with my dad; she loved him and chose to marry him, but never had that "this is the one" feeling. *I was different though.* I would know. Or would I? Maybe this "floating away on bubbles" feeling was just that: *a feeling.* Maybe it wasn't a good way to know whether or not someone was right for me.

After all, I had that bubbly "this is the one" feeling before, with other guys — guys I'd never even dated! Then after I started getting to know them, it quickly became clear they *weren't* "the one." Or, more often than not, they just ended up choosing someone else instead of me. How could I just "know" that multiple guys were "the one" for me before I even knew them? I shuddered at the thought, thanking God once again that He protected me from my silly heart, full of fickle emotions.

Maybe I'm putting too much pressure on myself, expecting to immediately know whether or not I'm supposed to marry him, I thought with a sigh of relief. *I always do that, don't I?*

Shadows splayed across the ceiling as I stretched my arms upward. *Maybe I can't know,* again an unwanted thought. *Maybe it has to do with making a wise decision, rather than immediately feeling that a guy is right for you. Maybe you have to get to know him before you know. Maybe you have to actually date the guy to find out if it would be wise to be serious with him, to discover if you truly love him.*

I twisted my wrists around in circles, watching their shadows dance on the ceiling. *I think Travis and I have potential to work, but it could also be an epic failure. How can I know that until I actually know him? I mean, we are dating with care; we aren't giving our hearts or bodies away, we are simply getting to know one another safely, purely. That must be okay.*

Maybe I *couldn't* know yet if he was "the one." Maybe there wasn't even such a thing as "the one." Maybe there were multiple people you could choose from, but whoever you married became your "one." Whatever the case, I better get busy getting to know him!

— what you've asked for —

That summer Travis and I attended Saturday night services with our friends Isaac and Traci at a local church. One such evening, standing in the auditorium-style theater, with the band rocking out to Hillsong tunes and the congregation absorbed in worship, the presence of God invaded my senses.

It was one of those epiphany moments when you no longer hear what the band is playing, no longer feel the seat behind you...as your sense of earthly reality fades away, your full awareness is absorbed in the words He's speaking over you — one of those moments when you know beyond a shadow of a doubt that you have just sensed the inaudible voice of God. And then you're left with nothing more to say, only possessing tears and a silent sense of awe.

This memory stands out for me because God almost never speaks to me in this way. Usually I only sense a confusing silence, or a gentle impression on my heart. But this moment of clarity came out of nowhere!

That Saturday night during worship, as everything faded away, God's inaudible voice whispered to my spirit — three times — "Tiffany, I have what you've asked Me for."

Gently, my spirit received the words. Though it could have meant anything, I knew deep down, even then, that He was talking about my future husband.

The next week, during my regular Sunday morning service at the DuPré's church, God spoke the same thing to me — three times: "Tiffany, I have what you've asked Me for." Again, somewhere deep down, I felt Travis was not what I'd asked for.

And yet I knew my heart. I knew how easily I could confuse emotions with convictions. Even when God spoke so clearly, and I knew it was Him, I still couldn't be sure of the application. Was He talking about Travis? Maybe it could have been about my job or ministry or home. It would have been all too easy to make a rash decision based on an emotional high, when sometimes the wisest thing to do is give it time and talk with people we trust. So once the moment faded, I simply couldn't be sure what He meant. The only thing to do was wait and let those words be tested by time.

— Seriously —

Thus began nine months of the most healing companionship I'd ever imagined. If Eric had a polar opposite, it would have been Travis. The first time I let loose my crazy, ridiculous, quirky self in front of him, I had to apologize. "I'm sorry. That was probably too much. I don't want to scare you away."

He looked at me in surprise. "Are you kidding?! I love when you're crazy! It's so much fun!" I couldn't believe my ears.

A few weeks later, during a moment of panic, we walked quickly through rows of corn behind his house, as I blurted out, "I don't love you right now, and don't know if I ever will. That's not fair to you. I'm afraid, and I don't know where this is going. I don't want to lead you on. I understand if you want to break up."

When he caught up to me he replied, "That's okay. Take your time. I still want to date you."

What was wrong with this guy? Why would he still want to date someone like me, someone who didn't know if she'd ever love him, and was scared to death of dating him?

One day he asked if I could stop over at his house, since I was driving that direction anyway. I texted back, "Sure, but just to warn you, I haven't showered today. Or yesterday. Or the day before. I have sweatpants and a hoodie on. No makeup. Hair not done. I look pretty gross."

He wrote back, "I'm sure you look great, but I'm excited to see YOU, not your makeup."

Ha, but he hasn't seen me yet, I thought to myself.

He greeted me outside. When I stepped out of the car he enveloped me in a hug and asked, "What are you talking about? You look amazing!"

"Seriously?"

"Yes, seriously."

Every way in which Eric made me feel I was not enough, Travis made me feel like I was more than enough.

— Sexy enough —

Weeks passed. Weeks that made me glad I'd said yes to Travis. Though the fear lingered, I also found incredible life spoken into me at every turn. He was quick to tell me how beautiful I was, how giving I was, how fun I was. It was like he called those qualities out of me and made them true by saying them. As I slowly believed his words, I felt beautiful, confident, and secure. Felt like the kind of girl that a guy could fall in love with — for the first time in my life.

Though my weight once again dropped too low, this time because of anxiety over the relationship, my mind's struggles with body image all but disappeared. I stopped staring into the mirror wishing away my flaws, stopped hating my crooked face and too-small butt. Every time I felt unlovable or undesirable, Travis showed me another person: someone very beautiful at her worst moments, and someone generous at her most selfish times.

One evening, our friends Isaac and Traci joined us for a delicious homemade coffee-encrusted steak at my apartment. The two of them had just left as Travis slipped on his shoes.

During a brief hug goodbye, I kissed him. He kissed me back. My arms slipped around his neck, as his found my waist. His hair became tangled with my fingers. I couldn't get enough. I wanted him to want me. I tried to push him farther as I pulled him toward the couch. Minutes twisted into more than an hour. Every time we made out, I reached this point of unquenchable desire. Seductive power coursed through me; seeing the desire in his eyes made me feel beautiful enough, sexy enough, and *good enough*.

Out of nowhere, Travis' hands flew up and locked around my wrists. Picking himself up, he stalked to the other side of the room, running his hands through his hair. "Tiff, we have to stop."

I jumped up, biting my lip. Slipping behind him, I tried to kiss his back through the soft cotton shirt that smelled of cologne.

"Stop." He whirled around, took my arms again, and gently plopped me back onto the couch, holding me there at arm's length. Kneeling in front of me, he held my gaze with earnest intensity. "Tiff, I'm trying to treat you like a daughter of the King. I respect you, I care for you. I know we shouldn't be doing these things. I know you'll feel guilty about it tomorrow."

My heart spilled open. Memories tumbled into my mind: Eric asking me to pose like women he'd seen in sexy pictures. I posed, hoping to God he found me attractive enough. Eric comparing my body to other women's — always pushing me to go farther than I wanted to, physically. Eric saying I wasn't sexy enough, that I was like a doll rather than a woman.

"Tiff, it feels like you're trying to be sexy enough for me," Travis said, "like you're trying to prove something. But you have nothing to prove!" he tightened his grip on my arms ever so slightly, trying to see if I was understanding.

Flooding my mind were all the times I'd feared I wouldn't be enough sexually for the man I married, that he'd tire of me, and that he wouldn't be satisfied with me. The fear that I'd never keep his attention.

"Tiff, you have no idea how badly I want to keep going!" Travis searched my expression. "You are so incredibly attractive, but I have to treat you like the daughter of the King that you are." He kissed me tenderly on the forehead. "I need you to help me do that."

The memories broke away.

I never thought I was worth that kind of love. Never in my wildest dreams had I supposed a man would consider me worth waiting for, worth protecting in this way. Since I hadn't found myself worthy of that kind of man, I'd settled for second best. I'd allowed the few guys I had encountered to enjoy my body in a way that they shouldn't have.

And yet this man with quiet strength knelt before me and washed all the fears away with his words. I was enough; I was more than enough. I was desirable, but even more than that, I was worth waiting for.

He respected me like I'd never respected myself. And as I looked into his eyes, I knew I was ruined for anything less. Never again would I give my body away because I thought it would make me sexy enough. *Now I knew.* I was enough, and the kind of man I was looking for was a man with the heart of my heavenly Father.

— decisions —

We dated for nine months. Nine months to forget what loneliness felt like.

Coming home to my empty apartment no longer felt sad; it felt full. I didn't notice its emptiness when climbing into my big bed — I only noticed the feeling of joy. The companionship that I shared with Travis had replaced the loneliness. Each day ended with a phone call as we drifted to sleep. I slept soundly, without lying awake or daydreaming before falling into slumber. Life was too full to need imagination.

And yet, even in the beauty, something wasn't right. At first I couldn't place the missing piece, but soon it became apparent: *I'd never fallen in love with him.*

There had never been butterflies in my stomach when I saw him. Never a feeling of head over heels. There was comfort, but not an I-can't-imagine-life-without-you feeling. And there was no peace in my heart. Whether or not those bubbly emotions would come when I met the right person, the thing that made me wonder if I should be with Travis was that I never felt a peaceful confidence that I really wanted to be with him.

I created an "emo-lendar" (aka emotion calendar) to track my fluctuating emotions. Some days I wanted to spend my life with Travis: wanted to plan our wedding and wake up to him in the mornings. Other times I couldn't take one more day: I felt stifled, claustrophobic, and frustrated. After a couple months of tracking, I saw there was no pattern to the emotions. They didn't follow my PMS; they simply shifted day by day.

"Maybe I don't need to fall in love," I suggested to the DuPrés. "Maybe I can't fall in love anymore; maybe one shot was all I got."

"Have you ever told him you loved him?" Pastor Mark asked.

I shook my head. "No. Never. Because I don't know if it's true."

"Wow, after nine months? That's a big red flag," Mrs. DuPré said. "Are you letting yourself fall for him? Or trying not to?"

"I think I'm letting myself. I pray and try to love him. I just *can't*. Not like that." And I wasn't referring to bubbles in my stomach; I was lacking peace in my heart.

Mrs. DuPré shook her head. "If you can't fall in love with him, don't marry him."

"Maybe now is the time to reevaluate your relationship," Pastor Mark added. "You've been together about nine months, which has given you some time to get to know each other and see if you're heading in the same future direction. Now is a good time to reevaluate. That way you won't date forever and look back one day wondering why you wasted years on a relationship, just because it was comfortable."

Pastor Mark met with Travis later that week and suggested we take a "change of pace." Though we would still be officially together (to avoid unnecessary drama), Travis thought it would be good to only talk once a week for a month. During our time apart, we would each pray and seek God about the future of the relationship.

"I don't like it, but I think it would be good. We should do it," Travis sorrowfully presented the idea to me.

That idea made me feel like I could breathe again, as though it were my chance to escape what had never felt fully right. "Yes, let's do it," I instantly responded.

— clarity —

Clouds chased each other across the darkening sky. Breezes sifted through my hair. Following my usual path, my feet fell ever onward. Such openness! I spread my arms as if about to fly and breathed deeply, filling my lungs with freedom. I was filling my spirit in this moment with the Divine.

"Tiffany, I have what you've asked Me for." The words returned to me on the wind in that first hour of our "change of pace." My answer before I'd prayed one prayer.

Stepping carefully over the cracks in the road, I remembered: our disagreements over finances, over the type of lifestyle we would live. Him with his dreams of a house in suburbia, white picket fence, 2.5 kids, good school district, nice possessions...all wonderful things. But then there was me: the girl who dreamed of being martyred in China and never once dreamed of owning a house or nice things (other than cute clothes, of course). Those disagreements would only escalate in marriage.

Then there was the fact that Travis was always encouraging me in my dreams, but never dreaming with me. He never had any real, personal interest for the things in my heart. Travis had said he'd travel with me if I started speaking full-time, but I knew that although he wasn't aware of it now, someday he'd resent me if he followed. I needed someone who would lead.

I smiled into the heavens: a smile of beautiful release. I filled my lungs with fresh air; with clarity, inspiration, and peace.

"I have what you've asked Me for."

Then, abruptly, darkness settled over me. Unlocking my door. Switching on the light. Finding an empty apartment. Having no one to call.

I forgot what loneliness feels like. Discarding my keys on the table, I walked numbly to the couch where Travis and I had sat so many evenings. *I forgot how oppressive the emptiness is.* Dropping onto the cushions, I curled up in the fetal position and wrapped my arms around my knees. *Hold yourself together, Tiffany. Hold yourself together.*

— left unspoken —

Five long, miserable days passed. During the sunlight, clarity came. I knew that despite the emptiness, I had to be alone. God had someone else for me.

During the night hours, sleep evaded me and loneliness stole my breath away. *How can I live like this? What is love anyway? Maybe love is to no longer feel lonely. Or maybe it's companionship, someone to share life with. Maybe we don't need to "fall in love," as long as we choose to love someone.*

Years ago I thought I had loved Eric, but from this new perspective, that kind of "love" was just a momentary "high" powered by insecurity and teenage obsession. It was surface infatuation, without any hint of real self-sacrifice. There were many times I thought I'd fallen "in love," but had I ever truly *loved* any of those people?

My mom said marriage was about giving 100% without expecting anything in return, and I didn't feel that way about anyone I'd met. But wasn't that kind of giving more of a choice rather than a feeling? Do you need to feel anything at all in order to love someone, to choose to serve them? So then, what was love? And could I love Travis?

When our first week apart ended, I rushed to dinner with trembling hands and an expectant smile. As soon as his arms wrapped around me, I felt whole. I was no longer alone in the world. I couldn't keep my hand from his all through dinner. Our eyes wouldn't unlock.

As he slipped away into the evening shadows, he touched his lips to my forehead. Its tenderness was beautiful. It made me feel cared for and respected — desirable and pursued. That moment he gave his heart away and told me what he never had, because I didn't want to hear it, and perhaps because he didn't fully know it himself. It told the words we had left unspoken: *He loved me.*

And that moment also told the words I hadn't fully realized: Yes, he was an absolutely incredible guy. Yes, I respected him. *But that didn't mean he was right for me.* That didn't mean I should be with him.

— new reflection —

Has anyone ever loved me this thoroughly, or deeply, or beautifully? I gazed into the mirror at a new reflection, one I'd never seen before Travis had showed her to me. *He makes me feel strong. Brave. Beautiful. Like someone who others can't help but fall in love with. Someone kind and generous. Someone beautiful beyond words.*

"I don't want to give him up," I whispered to the girl in the mirror. "I feel safe with him. He showed me what it's like to share life with someone, how good it can be. I don't want to let go because how can anyone else love me like that? He pursued me, and isn't that how a girl's heart is won?"

And yet, looking back into the eyes of this new girl, the one found through Travis, I couldn't tell if she was in love with him, or with the person he empowered her to become. The person he showed her that she already was.

— the moment —

The sun made puppet shadows of our entwined fingers. Swinging like a frayed lifeline, they held us together for dear life. Walking along the grassy meadow, we sensed the end of this beautiful day, this beautiful season. The end was about to find us in the sunset. Four weeks had flown past; too long for time apart, but too quickly for the chapter which was rapidly closing.

"I'm not that good at waiting," he laughed nervously, "so what are you thinking?"

"I...I was thinking..." I paused. *How do I say this? What if I am making a huge mistake I'll regret for the rest of my life? And how does one go about breaking up with someone she cares so much about...only she doesn't love him?*

"I think that we need to break up." I pushed the words out, popping the moment and shoving the chapter closed.

"I agree." He stopped walking and took me in his arms. I buried my head in his chest, this final embrace.

— altar —

The lock ground open on my door. Empty kitchen. Empty couch. Empty heart.

Tears began to slide down my cheeks and fog my glasses. Kneading my eyes, I fell on my bed, turning on soft music. Within minutes it felt like I was suffocating, like I couldn't breathe deeply enough to fill all the emptiness within.

I stumbled to my piano and began to play a new song I'd written. It was a declaration of faith. An altar of remembrance to who God is.

You could have been anything You wanted to be
You could have been high and far off, but instead
You chose to die for me
Thank You for being a God who is good
Thank You for being a God who is on our side

Tears rolled heavily down my cheeks and dripped off my arms, leaving salty trails in their wake. My voice croaked through the song of faith; at times I couldn't get the words out, and instead could only mouth them.

Throughout the years, an unformed question had hovered in the back of my mind: Was God holding out on me? Now I knew. *He wasn't.* He wasn't holding out on me, because He had already given me the greatest gift of all: *Himself.*[29]

It was beautiful. Instead of letting the emptiness overtake me, I remembered who my Father was, and it made me feel whole even in my brokenness.

> He wasn't holding out on me, because He had already given me the greatest gift of all: Himself.

— the grand finale —

Fourth of July rolled around again. That summer it was just me and my friend Traci at the fireworks, but I didn't feel

---

[29] *See Genesis 15:1, in which God dialogues with Abram, saying that He Himself is Abram's exceedingly great reward.*

alone. For once I felt full. Whole. Beautiful. Confident.

As rocket after rocket slipped into the air, I knew that God had something up His sleeve for me. Something or someone I couldn't see yet. This season felt like the quiet darkness that comes just prior to a brilliant explosion bursting before your eyes. All was quiet. All was peaceful. All was dark. But an incredible release was coming. One God had designed just for me. There was no doubt about it; this was the calm before the beautiful storm.

I lay back in the grass as the finale began, turning the night sky bright with color. Somehow, deep down, I knew that He had my back. Who could tell what was up His sleeve, but whatever or whoever it was, *I couldn't wait*. It was going to be an amazing adventure, and there was no place I'd rather be than adventuring with Him. Mesmerized by the sparkling lights bursting above me, I couldn't help but think:

Fireworks are like relationships. Some slow to start, some perfect fairytales. But mine…mine is going to be like the grand finale!

— pool party —

Six weeks had passed since the break-up, spring slipping into summer.

"Hey, Tiff!"

"Oh, Ryan, I'm so glad you're here!" Hugging my friend, I glanced around at cars lining the road. I'd gotten used to walking into parties with Travis beside me. "Can I walk in with you? I'm not sure how many people I'll know."

"Of course! Yeah, I think Moriah invited a bunch of her college friends too, so I'm expecting it'll be a lot of new faces." Ryan led the way around the garage. "How are things going with you and Travis?"

"It's been pretty good. I definitely miss it, but I think I miss the companionship more than I miss him, so it was probably a good choice to break up."

"I know he's pretty torn up about it," Ryan swung open the gate.

"Oh really? I still see him pretty regularly. We're friends and all, just not dating material."

"I understand how that goes."

"Ryan! Tiffany! I'm so glad you found it!" Moriah skipped across the deck. We rocked back and forth in a quick hug. "I think Travis is coming," she whispered into my ear. "That's not awkward, right? 'Cause you guys are still friends?"

I laughed, "Yeah, that's fine. No worries. Zero awkwardness."

"Okay, good. That's what Traci said you'd say. Here, want something to drink?"

I found an ice cold soda and made the rounds, meeting the new faces. As I joked with some of the girls I knew, Moriah screeched, "Yay, it's Traci and Isaac!" And there beside them, sun glinting off his blonde hair, came Travis. He had never looked so handsome as he did that afternoon, laughing his way into the party.

Travis followed Traci and Isaac up the deck stairs and stopped to give me a hug. Man, what was it about today? Was it the fact that I was no longer dating him that gave him new appeal?

"Hey, Tiff, look at this pool," Isaac nonchalantly swaggered over to its edge. "I wonder how deep it is."

"I'm not falling for that one. You're gonna push me in!"

Before I knew what was happening, Travis rushed over and threw me in the pool! Isaac shoved Traci in after me, sundress and all. We screamed bloody murder, but the pool party had officially begun.

A few hours later, wiping sweat from his forehead, Ryan looked up from the grill. "Burgers are ready!"

Traci and I joined the food line as I glanced back angrily at some chick chatting up Travis by the pool. *Did she not realize we'd just broken up?*

"You okay?" Traci asked.

"Oh yeah. I'm fine. Just so stinking mad."

"At least he's not flirting back." Apparently she was witnessing the same situation dancing before my eyes.

"Oh he's totally enjoying every minute of it!" I seethed. *Why did I break up with him?! I want to say he's mine tonight!*

Too many hours passed, eating up my stomach with feelings of inadequacy and jealousy. When the party finally dispersed, I did the unthinkable. I invited Travis to join Isaac, Traci, and me for a movie. I asked him to massage my back during the movie. I invited him back to my apartment afterwards. I kissed him, again and again. Because of my jealousy, I began playing with his heart all over again.

— whiplash —

Every other day I changed my mind. My changing emotions were giving me whiplash, let alone poor Travis! I wanted to be with him, then I didn't. Did, didn't. Did, didn't. At this point it should have been clear; if I was this confused and unsure of the relationship for months on end, I could be quite confident that I should end the relationship. It was good

> I forgot that God is bigger than all my fears.

that I'd given us a chance, but now, even in the confusion, I had my answer: We weren't supposed to be together. I was just afraid to let him go, afraid that I might end up alone, afraid that I might make the wrong decision. I was forgetting that God is bigger than all of those fears.

My 25th birthday was spent with Travis. Months came and went. I was caught up in the lust of the moment, pushing our physical boundaries farther. I gave no thought to respecting him or myself; instead I threw myself at him. Perhaps throwing my body at him would protect my heart.

"Tiffany." One night Joel and I were cooking a new recipe he'd found (chocolate smothered chicken of sorts) when he looked at me from the other end of the kitchen, "You can't do this to Travis. He loves you, but he won't tell you that because you don't want to hear it. This break has been really hard for him because he would do anything to become what you want him to be. He wants to have you in any way he can, even if that's just as a friend. You can't do this to him, because if you do, he won't be able to let you go."

Traci finally had enough too. Saturday night church had ended as we leaned against my little red hatchback, autumn's wind nipping at our faces. "I don't know what I want!" I moaned for the thousandth time. "Part of me wants to end it, but part of me is afraid that would be the biggest mistake of my life! I might regret it forever."

"Tiffany, this is not fair to him," Traci said. "You are not allowed to go on dates with him anymore or make any further decisions about this for three months. You need to distance yourself to see clearly. Come January, make the decision once and for all."

— faith —

Those three months passed quickly. I had stepped down to a part-time position at my job while completing my full-time graduate internship in music therapy at a hospital, along with my thesis work. Time flew from my fingers. Loneliness dissipated, as I was too tired to feel much of anything. Sinking into bed at night, I longed for companionship, but sleep came with sweet reprieve before there was time enough to sink into emptiness.

Those three months brought clarity as well. I didn't miss Travis; I missed *being with someone.*

One afternoon Joel came to watch our new favorite spy show. Setting down grocery bags of fruits and nuts, he started pulling dishes out of my cupboards. "So, Tiff, have you decided what you're going to do about Travis?"

"I don't think I miss him, but I do keep coming back to one question: Will I regret this for the rest of my life? He's a good man, Joel. A really good guy. Will I ever find someone else to love me the way he does?"

"If you knew you would find someone else, would you still date Travis?"

"No." There was no hesitation in my answer.

"Tiff, we are called to walk by faith, not by fear."[30] Crossing his arms, Joel leaned against the counter. "You're making this decision based on fear of the unknown, but God calls us to make our decisions based on faith. Faith that He is good and He knows our needs and He delights in us. Faith that He is able to do exceedingly abundantly above all we ask or think." He turned back to slicing the strawberries. "So make this decision based on faith, not on your fears."

— january decisions —

The pages of time turned onward yet again. *January.*

Pulling the homemade scarf higher around my neck, I slipped from my car into the bitter wind. *At least there's not much snow this year*, I thought, dreading the long winter months ahead. *Why does New York waste nine of its precious months on winter?*

Dashing across the parking lot, I swung open the door of the local coffee shop, the coffee-scented warmth and songs of Norah Jones extending a familiar invitation. Travis had asked me to meet him there that night, before our young adults group. I'd almost said no, still hadn't fully made up my mind as to what I would say. Waiting at the only open table, he jumped up and waved. I grinned and dropped my coat at the chair opposite him. "What can I get you?" he asked.

"No, no, I got it. Really. Thanks though." The last thing I wanted to do was make this seem like a date. "Can you watch my stuff while I order?" *Raspberry chai.* Yes, that would make me feel better. Liquid courage and liquid comfort all at once.

---

[30] *See 2 Corinthians 5:7, Galatians 2:20, and Galatians 3:11.*

After nearly an hour of small talk, Travis finally got to the point. "Now that it's January, I'm curious what you're thinking about us."

I could tell he was nervous from the way he laughed at nearly every sentence that escaped his lips. Setting down his coffee, he continued, "I still really care about you, and would like to get back together. Tiff...I've never told you this before, but...*I'm in love with you*. And I have been for a long time."

The walls seemed to fall inward. The room felt too full, too close. *What did he just say? After all these months of dating, these years of knowing him,* what *did he say?*

"I — I have to think," I stammered. "I don't know — don't know what to say." Shoot! I hadn't prepped for this, hadn't thought through my emotions. I thought we were just grabbing coffee to catch up after the holidays, not to have a relationship heart-to-heart! *What should I say?*

Okay, that wasn't true. Deep down, I had known he'd bring this up tonight; I just hadn't wanted to think about it. I'd wanted to bury my head in the sand, as I did with anything that seemed too confusing to handle.

"Umm..." I glanced at my phone. "Oh wow, we're going to be late for the meeting! We should probably go." I started gathering my things, looking for any excuse to get out, get away.

His eyes betrayed his disappointment. "Oh, sorry, I lost track of time."

I softened. "Can I get back to you on this? I just haven't thought it through yet."

"Sure, no problem." He tugged on his coat. "We better hurry so we're not too late. I'll see you there."

Slight specks of snow were falling silently as we escaped the overheated shop. I dove into my car. *What to do, what to do?* My fingers moved numbly over my phone keypad. Traci would already be at the meeting, but I had to send a quick SOS.

Church lay just down the road, and Travis walked in beside me. We were late, and made our way too obviously together toward the back. *Couldn't we just blend in? Why was everyone sitting already instead of mingling? And yet, this is nice. I like walking in beside a man. I like being a girl whose heart is spoken for.*

Traci slid her phone from her pocket and texted, "So what are you thinking?"

I looked around. We were in the far back of several hundred young adults. Pastor wouldn't notice; I didn't want to be rude, but I felt desperate. "I think I'm going to say no. Am I crazy?"

"You're not crazy," came the reply a few minutes later. "I think that's wise."

Slouched between Traci and Travis, deep peace filled me. Confidence. I would miss out on so much more if I stayed with Travis just because it was comfortable. The overwhelming realization came: *I'm not in love with him now, and I never will be.* It suddenly became crystal clear, no doubt in my mind. I didn't know yet how to find out if someone *was* "the one," but at least I knew that Travis *wasn't.* The answer was no. *I've been holding onto him out of fear of being alone,* I thought, *but like Joel said, I'm not called to walk by fear; I'm called to walk by faith.*

— the gift —

Travis and I talked after young adults. He walked me to my car, and I gave him my answer. Finally we had reached closure, reached the end.

As I drove home, numb loneliness overtook me. I prayed wearily into the darkness, "Lord, if you want me to stay single for a while, I will. But I need you to take away this overwhelming loneliness." Tears filled my eyes. "God, would you either send my husband or take the edge off this desire? I can't do what you've called me to do when I feel this loneliness. It's so overwhelming that it

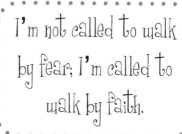

I'm not called to walk by fear; I'm called to walk by faith.

paralyzes me!"

It must have been the thousandth time I'd prayed that prayer over the years, but it was the first time anything changed. Never before had God changed my situation or emotions. Each time He'd called me to walk through the discomfort and loneliness. He'd called me to come closer to Him, to trust Him even when it was hard. He'd called me to honor Him, and trust that He would provide as I stayed surrendered to His will.[31] The words of Elisabeth Elliot had comforted me many times: *Loneliness is a required course for leadership.*[32] I'd hoped that somehow my singleness would be preparation for more to come.

But this time…this time was different. He took the edge off the desire. For the first time in my life, I *felt* content.

It was the weirdest thing! Had I been content before that moment? *Absolutely!* I'd already been living in contentment by surrendering my desires for years. The constant tension of surrendering my desires, of fighting for contentment, had produced far more growth than taking away the desire ever would have. The tension had shaved down my selfishness and impatience in certain areas of life, teaching me to trust my Father even when it wasn't easy. But this was the first time I'd actually

> The constant tension between surrendering my desires and fighting for contentment, produced far more growth than taking away the desire ever would have.

---

[31] See 1 Samuel 2:30, in which God says He will honor those who honor Him. See also Galatians 6:7, which talks about reaping what we sow. Are we sowing a life that honors God, or a life that is all about ourselves? When we honor God in our choices and lives, we can rest in the promise that God rewards those who diligently seek Him (Hebrews 11:6).

[32] Elisabeth Elliot. As quoted in Eric and Leslie Ludy, *When God Writes Your Love Story* (Sisters, OR: Multnomah, 2004), 150.

felt content. It was the weirdest experience to have my feelings line up with my beliefs, because that doesn't always happen in full. And yet, here I was, finally feeling what I'd already believed for a long time. Not because I'd arrived. It was simply...*a gift.*

I thought back to my long-ago nightmare of the handsome Adonis telling me exactly why I was still single. The pep talk I'd given myself in the mirror that morning: *Be happy, be happy, be happy; you want to be single!* The conversation with Jenna danced before my eyes, when she said I had to let God change me. *And He had.* This deep-rooted contentment was a gift. It was nothing I could have conjured up, nothing I could manipulate or force; *it was a gift.*

In that moment, inexplicable confidence took over my heart that He was holding in His hands everything I'd asked Him for, particularly with my future husband, just as He'd spoken to my heart months ago. But I also knew that even if I never married, I would still have more than enough in the greatest gift of all: *Christ Himself.*

— obvious changes —

A few days later at work, three of the students I supervised lounged in my office, filling me in on their latest love life developments. My favorite part of working at a college was talking with the students, getting to share a small portion of their lives.

Just before they left for class, one of the girls said, "We want to be like you, Tiffany."

"What are you talking about?" I asked, bewildered.

"You're so independent! You don't need a guy in your life to be happy. You know who you are. We want to be like that."

I couldn't believe my ears! My first interaction with Kelly, my college RA, flooded back into my mind. *How was she so happy and single?* Now these students were noticing the same thing in me. A smile spread across my face. *Praise God! This is something only He could ever do!*

Apparently this change inside me was more obvious than I imagined. This gift of contentment was changing everything. And apparently He had started changing everything before I even realized He was working, since the students had been noticing this contentment for a while. *How typical.* I was always the last to see the results when He'd been working major changes into my life.

— get up and do it —

January turned to February. Around a wobbly, old coffee table, I shared my life vision with several friends: Putting a team together. Speaking across the country. Raising money to open a free-of-charge center for girls struggling with eating disorders.

When I'd finished, my long-time visionary friend Nate said, "Tiff, it's not time for that yet. Right now, you need to get off your butt and finish writing your book."

I went home and wrestled with that. Nate had always been on board with my vision in the past, so why not this time? I felt betrayed. And then, slowly, it dawned on me that he was right. I'd been waiting for a magical word from God telling me that The Insatiable Quest for Beauty was finished and ready to be released. Well, sometimes God works through other people. *So I got off my butt and finished it.* Pulling together a focus group of incredible friends, we hashed through each chapter together. I completely scrapped and rewrote multiple chapters based on their feedback. That spring, amidst my internship, job, and thesis work, I spent hours upon hours writing and editing. The same week of graduation, I submitted the final copy to print.

— miracle of miracles —

The basement of the arena echoed with excitement. Anticipation bounced off the walls as students re-pinned graduation caps to their heads and shuffled around in long, flowing robes.

Commencement. In one hour the past four years of evening classes after work would be worth it, and I would hold in my hand an official certificate from the college: *My master's degree.*

Robes billowing around me, I followed amidst the throngs of students arranged in perfect symmetry. Mom, Dad, and the grandparents were upstairs somewhere, watching from the bleachers. Dad, always the observant one, would spot me somehow and manage a picture or two before we sat in our pre-arranged rows.

This time maybe my cap would even stay on my head. I'd triple bobby-pinned it after my bachelor's graduation, when it fell off as I went to shake the president's hand.

I'd already been to my fair share of graduations. There was my home school graduation when Eric barely skated in in time, and I felt unwanted, desperately waiting for him to show up. Then my associate's graduation during a week day just after Eric and I broke up, when I had to ride the bus back to my parked car and drive home alone, never having felt more lonely in my life. There was my bachelor's graduation when I felt overwhelmingly sad, longing for a man to share the moment with me and meet my family. Not the best memories of graduations, so as you can imagine, the only reason I came today was for my mom's sake.

Honestly, the best part was watching the undergraduate students. I'd known many of them through my job at the college, some since their first year. Now seeing the glow on their faces, the anticipation of this chapter's end, filled me with joy. When my name was called at long last, I grasped my certificate with a beaming face.

After the ceremony, I snaked my way through hard-packed crowds of parents and students, finally finding my family across the street. Stripping off my robe to reveal coral skinny jeans, I posed for picture after picture before suggesting we find somewhere to eat. *I was starving!*

It wasn't until the next week that the miracle of that day hit me: *I hadn't once remembered the fact that I was single!* My jaw literally fell open at the realization. No thought of wanting a boyfriend, no awareness of my single status; *it simply hadn't crossed my mind.* Driving down the highway, I sat in wordless awe at what God had done.

— do you trust me now? —

Two weeks after graduation, the first 150 copies of The Insatiable Quest for Beauty were waiting on my doorstep, literally just in time for that night's conference. Unsure of what to expect at my first ever vendor table, I wrote the cost with lipstick on a mirror: $7 each or two for $12.

They went like hot cakes. I sold nearly all of them that weekend, bringing in more than enough income for the month's rent and electric bills.

My life felt like the Verizon commercial, in which people are walking all over town asking into their phones, "Can you hear me now? Can you hear me now?" and the answer is always yes, because it's Verizon. I felt like God was asking me His version of that commercial: *Do you trust Me now, Tiffany? With finances? With singleness? With your future? How about now?*

As I carried the few merchandise remnants back to my car, I thought: *If this is where walking by faith leads, then I will walk by faith forever.*

BOY TALK

THE SEX TALK

Travis and I set physical boundaries in our relationship, to help us make wise choices. I knew it was wrong to have sex before marriage,[33] and still never have, but I tend to get too close to that line in an attempt to keep a guy's attention. That's an area of brokenness God is healing inside me, which creates an even greater need for clear boundaries. Here are some boundaries the DuPrés talked about with Travis and me. Maybe they'll give you some ideas too!

1) Plan your dates. Don't spend too much time alone together, and if you are alone, spend time in public places. (Typically people do not throw themselves across a Starbucks table in order to make out in front of the baristas, so public places help minimize temptation.) In other words, hanging out for long amounts of time alone in your apartment or bedroom isn't a great idea. Also think about how late you stay out. Being tired is like being drunk; you lose some of your inhibitions and logical thought processes. Plan for that. At the beginning of an evening spent with your boyfriend, decide when the date will end, so neither of you will feel rejected when you part ways. If there's no plan, it's too easy to carry the date on forever or begin getting too

---

[33] *See 1 Corinthians 7, among other passages.*

physical, worrying that your significant other will feel rejected if you decide to leave. Plan where you're going and have people who know when to expect you home, as a built-in source of accountability. That is how to set yourself up for success, instead of setting yourself up for failure.

2) Celebrate sex! Yup, you heard me right! Part of celebrating sex is to guard it like a treasure. In this case, that means protecting it for the right time and place. Just as you hopefully wouldn't have sex in the middle of a shopping mall filled with people (awkward), so we should celebrate God's gift of sex by saving it for the context for which it was created! And let me tell you...I am SO EXCITED to get to experience this gift when I get married! Most of my life I've looked at physical purity as a series of rules, most of which said, "Hands off!" It's only been recently that I've begun to search out the joy and reward of staying pure physically. It's a total perspective shift! Instead of just avoiding messing up, I look to see how fully I can honor God in my physical relationships. When we truly believe God is good, it's easier to obey Him, because we know that following His way brings life.[34] When we get too physical before marriage, it is setting ourselves up to be hurt, and God wants to protect us from that. Sex is designed to be celebrated in a marriage relationship, in which both people are committed "til death do us part."[35] Outside of marriage, it becomes a tie to another person who may exit our lives at any time. My friend Andrea has been married for a couple decades, and told me that one of the reasons she trusts her husband so much is because he honored marriage before he was even married. He was trustworthy in the way he treated her physically while dating, and so she trusts him even more now that they are married. What a beautiful picture of the way we can celebrate sex even while single!

---

[34] See Psalm 16:11, Psalm 24:3-5, Psalm 91:14-16, Proverbs 19:16, Matthew 16:24-27, and John 15:9-11, among other passages.

[35] "Honor marriage and guard the sacredness of sexual intimacy between wife and husband...." (Hebrews 13:4, The Message translation)

3) Have realistic expectations of sex. I know, that blows my mind too. See, I've built sex up in my imagination to be this absolutely incredible experience that I can't even wait to explore! And I'm sure it will be wonderful (though from what I hear, sometimes it may seem a bit overrated if we've built it up in our minds to be this out-of-body caliber of experience every time), but somehow marriage has become all about sex in my mind, when really...it's about so much more! Married friends tell me that even though they really enjoy sex, it isn't always a mind-blowing experience. It's different than what they waited for. Marriage itself is about sharing life with someone and incredible intimacy; the physical side of things is only one part of that intimacy. When we build up sex to be the one thing we are waiting for, we set ourselves up for disappointment, and set up our future marriage to be built on a shaky foundation.

4) Set boundaries. I don't want to lay down specific rules about what you should or shouldn't do physically with your boyfriend, because I can't find those rules in Scripture, besides the rule of simply not having sex until marriage. Besides, my goal isn't to be legalistic; it's to honor God. When you set boundaries, I strongly encourage you to talk with adults you trust to see what they suggest, and pray about it. Some boundaries Travis and I set were to keep our clothes on, and not to touch anywhere we couldn't see (in other words, if clothes are covering it, don't touch it). The temptation was to just wear scantier clothing, but I had to keep refocusing my perspective to honor God in all my actions, rather than to see how far we could go. I have friends who have set a wide variety of boundaries, all the way to not even kissing before their wedding day! That's not my personal conviction, but if it is yours, I encourage you to give it your all. If one of you has more conservative boundaries than the other, go with the more conservative boundaries, so both your hearts are pure toward God.[36] Seek God, follow your conscience, and talk with people you trust about your boundaries, because even what we

---

[36] *See Romans 14.*

perceive as our conscience can be hardened by society. It can feel totally natural to have sex with someone you're not married to, but that doesn't make it right. Talk with trusted adults about your boundaries, because we are easily deceived into thinking that whatever feels good or natural in the moment is also wise and right, and that's not true.

5) Keep a healthy distance from the "line" physically. A physical relationship is meant to build up to something; there's always this tension of wanting to go further than the last time. When you set boundaries, I encourage you not to immediately try everything, because then there's nowhere to build to. If you take things slowly, you can build up to your boundaries over time. Getting super physical also makes it hard to decide whether or not a person is good for you, because it clouds your judgment. It's hard to tell (at least for me) whether you really like the *person*, or whether you really like *making out* with him. Physical chemistry is definitely important, but is not a solid foundation for a relationship.

6) Ask, "Where is my temptation coming from?" When you are tempted to go too far physically (which, if you're anything like me, will be a temptation), ask yourself, "Where is this temptation coming from? What am I thinking, and why am I doing this?" Are you trying to prove something or be sexy enough? Do you feel insecure? Are you trying to fill a need inside? Are you trying to show you love the other person? Take those reasons to God, and ask Him how you can fill them in a pure way. For example, what are other ways you can show your boyfriend you care about him? Or how can you turn to God instead of to a physical relationship to help you feel secure? Even if you're well within your boundaries, be self-aware and conscious of your motives in the way you interact with your boyfriend.

7) Communicate honestly and regularly. Share your expectations and boundaries with each other. Instead of playing games, be up front and honest, and check in with each other on a regular basis. Which reminds me: *Guys don't get hints.* Like, *not at all.* I remember Eric asking if he could skip one of my concerts for a band rehearsal and I said, "Fine," in this steely voice that obviously meant it was not fine at all. I hung up the phone, whirled around, and said, "Dad, if he doesn't come, we're over!" My dad asked, "Did you tell him that?" My response was, "No, he can figure it out!" My dad said, "He's a guy. He can't figure that out. You need to tell him straight up." It's true. Guys have no idea. Instead of playing games, just be honest. When you have this conversation about boundaries, share your feelings and convictions in a kind, clear, and respectful way.

I thank God that by His grace I will have sex for the first time on my wedding night. Throughout the years I've often felt like the odd one out. In high school I felt like the only one who'd never had a boyfriend; as an adult I felt like the only one who was a virgin. But I realized that we weren't made to fit in; we were born to stand out.[37] I'm so thankful for the pain He's protected me from, the pain that would have come from having sex with my ex-boyfriends. When we choose His way, it leads to fullness of joy.

That being said, I definitely wasn't perfect and didn't always stick with the boundaries I set in relationships. Sometimes I looked at guys only through lust; sabotaging the relationship from the get-go by making it all about the physical side of things, never getting to know them beneath the surface. There were times when I felt like too much of a failure for God's grace. I don't know your story, but the amazing thing is that God's forgiveness is far greater than all of our brokenness and sin. He heals and restores our hearts and bodies, and has good things ahead when we surrender to Him.

When I started dating Travis, I realized he was worth waiting for. I wanted to protect our relationship, not sabotage it by getting too physical too fast. But the even greater revelation to me personally was this: No matter

---

[37] I love the quote, "Why are you trying so hard to fit in, when you were born to stand out?" [A Cinderella Story, directed by Mark Rosman (USA: Warner Bros.), 2004.] I love this quote because of verses like these: Romans 12:1-12, 1 Corinthians 6:12-20, and 1 Peter 2:9.

where we've been or what we've done, we are daughters of the King, which means that you and I are worth waiting for too.

DISCUSSION QUESTIONS

Use these questions as part of a small group, with a mentor, or on your own. As you prayerfully reflect on these, feel free to journal your thoughts in the spaces below each question.

1) Do you see yourself as worth waiting for? In what ways? How can you first and foremost honor God, and secondly honor yourself and your significant other in your physical relationship?

_____

_____

_____

_____

2) Someone once told me that the person we date could be our future spouse, but if not, then they'll be someone else's future spouse. Therefore, we should conduct ourselves in dating relationships the way we'd want another girl to treat our future husband. I think this is hard to understand before marriage. Sometimes I've thought, "Well, who really cares? It won't bother me if my husband's done all this stuff with some other chick first." But married friends have told me that when

you meet the person you want to spend your life with, suddenly it does matter in a whole new way. And even more importantly, it matters to God. So if you have a boyfriend, do you treat your physical relationship as though he could be someone else's husband one day?

_____

_____

_____

_____

3) Have you ever tried to be sexy enough for a guy? What do you think about Travis' perspective on that?

_____

_____

_____

_____

4) Even before God gave me the "gift" of feeling content (like I talked about earlier), I would say I had already become content. How? Simply by choosing to live that way and surrendering my will to His, in the midst of overwhelming desires. The feelings of contentment were simply a gift from God. I never could have manipulated myself into lessening that overwhelming longing for marriage. What do you think

about these things? How are you learning to be content?
What gifts has God given you to help?

_____

_____

_____

5) Have you ever stayed in a relationship because you were
afraid to be alone? In what ways (particularly regarding
boys) are you walking by fear? In what ways are you
walking by faith? How can you choose to do more of your
walking by faith?

_____

_____

_____

_____

6) Have you ever played with a guy's heart, like I did?
Maybe it's because of jealousy, like with me and Travis, but
there are many other reasons, such as to make us feel good
about ourselves or to win approval from our friends. How can
you recognize that you're playing with someone's heart?
How can you stop?

_____

_____

_____

_____

7) I shared a lot of my thoughts about "what is love?" and the idea of finding "the one." What do you think about these things? Do you think there's a "one" for each of us? Why or why not? Do you think "falling in love" is a feeling, a choice, a mixture of the two, or something else entirely? What does it mean to love someone?

_____

_____

_____

_____

8) I am so thankful for Joel's friendship in my life. Having good guy friends is so healthy, and allows us to offer a different perspective for each other. Who are the guys in your life that are good friends and/or role models for you? Are those relationships healthy? How can you build healthy friendships specifically with guys?

_____

_____

_____

_____

7 SINGLE AND SANE

AGE: 17 18 19 20 21 22 23 24 25 26

"Tiffany, why are you working full-time?"

My mom and dad were perched at our kitchen table back home, smiling into their laptop. My Skype account kept freezing — as did my back, which was leaning against a piano bench.

Six weeks ago I'd graduated with my master's degree in music therapy, and released <u>The Insatiable Quest for Beauty</u>: my first book, the one I'd dreamed of and worked on for years! I'd quit my job at the college in an attempt to free up more time for speaking, only to discover that I needed a job to make ends meet. After dozens of applications, I found myself stuck in a dead-end job that hardly paid the bills, and all for what? I still didn't have time to speak.

"I think you should quit your job and travel with your book. Just try it for a year. See what happens." As the words came out of my dad's mouth, a flutter of electricity jolted through my chest. *He was joking. No way he was serious.*

"Wait, are you serious, honey?" my mom asked doubtfully, always the realist of the duo. My dad the dreamer, my mom the realist. Completely opposite yet both completely practical.

"Yes, I am," dad defended his idea. "She can move all her things home to our house and then stay with family and friends across the country, canvassing each city to let them know about her book, speaking everywhere she can. After all, what does she have to lose? A dead-end job that she hates. An apartment and church she could return to at any time. And she's single."

My heart nearly leapt out of my chest! It felt like a lock clicked open on the door to my destiny. *This is it!* Cautious certainty filled my lungs. *This is what I've been waiting for all my life!*

And then it hit me in full color: *This is why I'm still single!*

— three weeks —

Three weeks to make a life-altering decision. If I wanted to start traveling that fall, I had to get ready. If I didn't want to pay an extra month's rent, I had to move out.

Hurriedly I set up meetings with my mentors and closest friends. Each time I shared the idea, grins split their faces as they replied without hesitation, "Yes, this is absolutely right. The potential is huge; this is totally a God idea. We stand behind you."

I dared to dream…and then hesitated.

One night, wrapping myself in the afghan I'd crocheted for my friend Traci, I asked, "Do you think I'm crazy? What am I doing? I haven't been able to sleep because I want to cry every night! I'm leaving everything I know: my friends, my home church; I feel alone already. I know I'll feel even more alone as I travel by myself. As much as this is what I've dreamed of, now that it's here I know it isn't going to be easy. I have to be sure this is the right decision."

Traci listened patiently, and then with her characteristic honesty, replied, "Tiffany, it will be sad if you leave, but it will be even more sad if you chicken out and don't do what God has put in your heart to do."

She was right. All of my life had been covert preparation for this moment. Just as Elisabeth Elliot said, this loneliness had been preparation for leadership.[38] Esther 4:14 played on repeat in my mind: "For if you keep silent at this time, relief and deliverance will rise for the Jews from another place, but you and your father's house will perish. And who knows whether you have not come to the kingdom for such a time as this?"[39] God could have used anyone, but He heard all the prayers I'd prayed: "God, fix your eyes on me! Send me. I will go anywhere, do anything, only please be glorified through me. I want to change the world with you. I want to be a history maker."

Now He'd placed this opportunity before me. Destiny stood before my eyes, as things I'd never understood (things like my singleness) suddenly made sense.

For such a time as this.

"You're right," I whispered, half to Traci and half to God. "I have to do this."

I told my landlords I was moving out, put in my two week's notice at work, and began giving away household items and taking carloads of belongings back to my parents' house in Albany, NY, four hours away.

That weekend I stood in church, drinking in my second-to-last Sunday in Rochester, aching already for the separation that was coming. In the middle of worship, the presence of God invaded my senses, saturating my mind. In an instant all I knew was His inaudible voice, more real than the words sung on stage, as He said, "You are about to stand in awe of Me."

Tears rolled down my face as I sank into my seat with the kind of joy that comes only when we reach the end of ourselves and find all of Him. In that moment I knew beyond a shadow of a doubt that this was His path for me. And my heart fluttered to life.

---

[38] Elisabeth Elliot. As quoted in Eric and Leslie Ludy, *When God Writes Your Love Story* (Sisters, OR: Multnomah, 2004), 150.

[39] *The ESV translation.*

— in its time —

It happened so fast, it didn't feel real. It was like all my life had been spent in the waiting room where He was quietly — all but invisibly — training me, and now He was saying *go*, and I was supposed to go. *Right away.*

Years ago while reading Isaiah 60, verse 22 had stopped me in my tracks as God spoke of fulfilling His word to Israel. The verse said, "...in its time I will do this swiftly."[40] Another translation put it this way, "...when it is time, I will make these things happen quickly."[41]

And isn't that how God works sometimes? Waiting. Waiting. And not just waiting, but waiting with *no prospects*. And then...the starting shot is fired and we are told to run.

— able —

Groaning and shoving with all the force I could muster, I strained to coerce the queen-sized mattress into the back of the minivan. My dad had helped me pack and transport most of my belongings the day before, but wasn't able to drive back out to Rochester for the last load. My friends were at work, as I hadn't anticipated the second trip, so I had to move the rest of my belongings all by my lonesome.

"God, I can't do this!" I prayed, close to tears from the physical exertion. "It won't fit, and I have to have it out by tomorrow! Please help me! Please send someone to help!"

A few minutes later, as I continued to wrestle with the mattress, a car pulled up and a man in his early 30s stepped out. "Can I help?" he offered, rolling up his shirt and putting his tattoo-sleeved muscles to work. *The first of many divine interventions.*

---

[40] *The NIV translation.*

[41] *The NCV translation.*

Together we barely managed to twist the mattress into the van. I thanked the man profusely, wiping sweat from my forehead, still shaky from holding in tears, as I thought: *Stepping out by faith is like shoving this mattress into the car. It's ridiculously hard. It feels impossible. Staying single for what seems to be "no reason" is like shoving a mattress into a car. It's painful and exhausting.*

As I wiped sweaty hands on my jean shorts, I thought: *When God gives us something that's difficult to do, He doesn't make it easier. Instead, He makes us able.*

— what ifs —

My 26th birthday presented itself the weekend after I moved home. I hadn't planned anything special, figuring I would spend time with my family, who I hadn't seen much of within the last year. I woke up early to go garage sale shopping with my mom, and then laid down for a noon-time siesta. When I awoke, loneliness settled on me like a winter coat. I tried to shake it off, but I couldn't move the overwhelming feelings of heavy-heartedness.

> When God gives us something difficult to do, He doesn't make it easier. Instead, He makes us able.

As I slowly stood, lies began to attack me with fury: *You have to choose between following your dreams or getting married. What if you end up single forever because you followed your dreams? You don't want that, do you?*

Dragging my laundry basket down to the basement, I swatted at the thoughts like flies, but they only grew more intense. *You can't have both marriage and your dreams! Which do you want more?*

Pulling sopping wet clothes out of the washer, I hung them roughly on hangers, trying to put away the thoughts with the clothes. *It's either dreams or marriage,* the torment continued. *Which will you choose?*

"Jesus, help me!" I whispered into the mustiness, there by the clothes line.

Immediately the thought came to my spirit: *"God never asked me those questions, so I don't have to answer them."*

In that instant, the questions ceased. I'd always wondered about my future, worrying about making the perfect decision. Back while transferring from the community college, I worried that going to one college instead of another would cause me to miss meeting "the one." I wondered if I hadn't dated Eric, would I have met someone else that year. But now I realized, all the "what-if" questions I'd asked about my past and future did not have to be answered. I couldn't know the answers, and in this moment, I didn't have to choose marriage or dreams, because God wasn't asking me to make that choice. All He was asking me to do was follow His lead right here and right now, leaving my future to Him. As a friend once told me, I wasn't called to understand; I was called to follow.

> God never asked me those questions, so I don't have to answer them. All He is asking me to do is follow His lead right here and right now, leaving my future to Him.

How many times had I prayed to know the future, begged God to tell me how long I would have to wait to get married? Now, on my 26th birthday, I thanked Him that He hadn't told me. It would have been too much for me to carry; I would have settled for the next decent guy who seemed semi-interested in me. I couldn't have imagined staying single for this long!

But now, everything was different. *Thank you that I'm single*, I breathed, letting go of the weight of the world in that one small breath. *You knew what you were doing, even though I didn't have a clue. Thank you for holding my future, instead of telling me what it held. For keeping me on your path instead of giving me what I asked for. I wouldn't have my life any other way. Truly this is better than my wildest dreams.*

> Thank you for holding my future, instead of telling me what it held.

John 13:7 meant more to me now than it ever had: "Jesus answered him, 'What I am doing you do not understand now, but afterward you will understand.'"[42] Now I could look back and understand the smallest portion of God's reasons why He'd kept me single, and even that drop of the ocean was enough for me to give thanks with all my heart.

— all in all —

Me, God, and my little PT Cruiser. Through six weeks of that fall semester we trundled across the mid-west, keyboard, guitar, and boxes of books jammed into my hatchback. I spoke in coffee shops and churches, high schools and colleges. Anywhere that would have me. Every need I encountered along the way, God met a hundred times over.

When I got a flat tire, pulled into the gas station, and didn't know what to do — someone pulled in after me and said, "Let me fill your tires. Looks like you have a nail in this one. Here's the name and address of a good mechanic."

When my laptop began to rapidly die, I prayed for a new one. As I was praying, a friend texted me, saying,

---

[42] *The ESV translation.*

"You're on my heart. Is there anything you need right now?" I told her I was keeping an eye out for a laptop. A few days later she and other members of my church family sent money to buy a new laptop.

His provision astounded me.

In January 2013, Traci and I drove from New York to Los Angeles, amidst blizzards, foggy Grand Canyons, and 17-hour driving days. She flew home from LA, while I spent the next five months avoiding winter by traveling to the western and southern states, watching God open up door after door.

Every few weeks, strangers came up me saying, "God's put on my heart that this is just the beginning for you. You haven't even started running yet. Figuratively speaking, God's going to give you new shoes, and you're going to run. And you have no idea how to move into that next season, but you don't have to know. He's going to take you there, and you don't have to do a thing."

It was like a dance. He led and I responded. I didn't have to figure out the next move, because He already had.

> It was like a dance. He led and I responded. I didn't have to figure out the next move, because He already had.

Through the lonely nights and monotonous drives, He was so close to me. *So close.* It seemed the very air I breathed housed His presence, His divine intervention, His destiny. When tingles of fear crept up my spine, His peace surrounded me.

Never before had I relied on Him for everything: Protection, provision, comfort, companionship, wisdom, peace...*everything. He became my all in all.*

— strangely satisfied —

All those moments I asked God to prepare my future, I pictured the man who would stand beside me at the altar. I pictured a stunning white dress (with pale pink accents) flowing behind me down the aisle. When I read Psalm 37[43] and began delighting in the Lord, I thought He would first fill the desire of my heart for marriage. Never had I pictured this:

Speaking across the country. Hearing stories of lives transformed and set free. Leading worship and sensing the presence of God so strongly. Having my heart beat more for the Lord and more for this ministry than it did for marriage. And all the while...single. Very much alive, and very much single. I felt sure that God would provide a marriage relationship someday, probably ten years down the road, but even if He didn't, I was also sure that *I would be okay.*

Marriage would be wonderful in its own way, but it would also be nothing like this. One can't be better than the other, because they're just different. So different. And I would never have this time of life back again, not like this.

As I opened the door and peered into the beginning of my destiny, everything within me felt whole and full and awake, like I had never felt in any relationship. I thought, *Maybe a relationship fills many people, but I would never have felt this full from a relationship. I wouldn't give up this adventure in order to marry young, but I would postpone marriage for this adventure. I'll wait as long as it takes, because right here, right now, I've found my destiny. And nothing satisfies quite as much as walking into the destiny God has for us. In this season, that includes singleness.*

Glimpses of the past few years flashed through my eyes: Working on my book. Recording a CD. Finishing my master's degree. Mentoring young women. Speaking in small groups and at conferences. Those were the moments that most filled me. Those moments made me far more alive

---

[43] *"Take delight in the Lord, and he will give you your heart's desires." (Psalm 37:4, NLT translation)*

than my most memorable dates and longest daydreams. In doing what I was made to do, my heart was strangely satisfied.

— what victory looks like —

As my five months of perpetual spring drew to a close, I took a weekend aside to enjoy an up-and-coming women's speaker via live internet broadcast. I watched, hidden in the back of the church auditorium, behind all the other women watching the broadcast on the front screen.

"Everyone God has healed of a physical ailment, stand up!" The speaker motioned for the audience to rise and shielded her eyes against the stage lights to search the room. "These people are witnesses to God's healing power; witnesses to His victory."

The audience began to cheer, unsure of what came next.

"Now," the speaker continued, "anyone praying for a healing, raise your hand."

Hands shot up all over the room.

"I want those who have been healed to pray for those who need a healing. You are witnesses to His victory!"

Next the speaker asked those who had been emotionally healed to stand and pray for those with broken hearts. Then, those who had experienced financial miracles to pray for those struggling with finances. On and on it continued in this fashion, until her grand finale: "All of those women who waited for the husband God had for them, and are now married, stand up!"

Beyonce's song "All the Single Ladies" popped into my mind as the single ladies in the audience went wild! When it was their turn to stand, they literally sprung out of their seats! I didn't stand, yet a sweet married lady came over to pray for me anyway. Though I appreciated her prayers, I couldn't help thinking:

Shouldn't I also be praying for my fellow single ladies? I mean, it's so nice that they are praying for us, but could we be missing the point? Have I been missing the point all these years? Because the end goal is not to be married; the end goal is to be content in any situation, whether hungry or full, single or married, poor or rich, sick or healthy. It's not whether or not our situation has changed that makes us a victor; it's whether or not we've learned contentment. More than being healed or married or anything else, surrender in the midst of desire is the truest testimony. And yet even more than learning contentment, the end goal is Jesus Himself. In all of life, He is our only goal.

Marriage? Healing? Financial provision? Those are only byproducts, if He so desires to give them. He Himself, and He alone, is our journey's end.

Even in singleness, my adventure had already begun, and victory was already mine.

> Surrender in the midst of desire is the truest testimony.

— adventures —

One of my final stops that spring was Nashville, TN. With wild red hair and lovable quirkiness, the lady sitting opposite me at a friend's church didn't know a thing about me except my name. Yet here she was sharing something God put on her heart for me which struck a chord in my soul: "I have this picture of you and God. You're wearing a backpack; you've already started off on an adventure together."

My mind flashed back to the image God had put in my heart years ago, just before I dated Eric: me bowing before three crosses on a hill, before the impending sunrise. *Just me and God.*

And then my mind snapped to a new picture of myself, this time with a backpack strapped on, following the Lord up a mountainside stream beneath a tangle of trees. Light filtered through the branches.

"The adventure is nowhere near over," the redhead continued. "He has so much more that He wants to show you! And He will provide all your needs as you come to them along the way."

Anticipation sifted through me, thinking of the sights we had left to see. *Just me and Him.* I could almost imagine the Lord pointing forward through the branches, like a guide familiar with the trail and excited to show off its beauty, then turning back to smile at me.

"It's so clear in this picture I have that it's just you and God on this adventure. It's *supposed to be* only you and God right now."

It clicked for me, settled into my spirit like the warmth of summer. Yes. Just yesterday I'd been praying about this, filled with a deep sense that my Father-daughter time was not yet complete. There was more to be shared on this adventure with just me and God. Much more.

Without realizing it, this lady with the quirky red hair had nailed it, fully confirming what God had already whispered to my heart: *My singleness was not yet complete; this season was not yet finished.* My Father was jealous for my heart, anticipating all the adventures He held in mind for us. Adventures I couldn't fathom, couldn't imagine, couldn't hold in my wildest daydreams.

And it was just beginning. We had only just set out, and there was so much more to come! *All He asked was that I stay close to Him.* In that closeness I would find the intimacy of my dreams, the companionship I'd craved.

I held this picture in my mind: *My Father and I exploring the mountains, watching the sunsets together. One day in the future we would emerge on the other side of the range, coming down out of the forest into a rich and luscious valley. I fully believed that I would see him there, the man waiting to join our journey. Our duo would become a trio. And together we would continue to venture further into new territory, walking on high places.*

But for once in my life, I was in no hurry to reach that valley. I prayed for that man when I thought of him, as I always had. I prayed he would be waiting there with his bags packed when we arrived. But in the meantime, I discovered that there's not room enough in a human heart to absorb all the adventures God has for us, much less put words to them. I could never contain every sight, every whisper, every sound of love in this mountain forest adventure with my Father.

— then there was austin —

I came home from my first tour in May, full of moments shared with my Savior, and anticipation for the next journey. I settled into prep work for Tour #2, and then...*then there was Austin*. The unfinished part of my love story. The one I had never quite forgotten.

He called me up one night, this sense of urgency in his voice. "What are you doing right now?" What was I doing? Well, I'll tell you what I *hadn't* done. I hadn't showered. No makeup. No cute clothes. Not exactly the "let's talk" look I'd usually go for. But I had waited ten years for this talk, and if he was ready, well I was more than ready.

We met at the Starbucks near my parents' house. I led the way across the plaza's parking lot, toward a side path weaving along a stream. Before we reached the path, he'd already blurted out, "Okay, if we have this conversation, it won't hurt our friendship, right? Because I don't want to lose you. I don't want this to change everything if it doesn't work out."

"I promise," I grinned lopsidedly. "However, you do realize that if one of us marries someone else, it will change everything. It's about time we stop being afraid of that. Eventually things are going to be different. We may as well talk about this and risk losing the inevitable a little early."

"That's true. I just don't want it to happen yet." He drew his hand over his face and took a deep breath. "Tiff, the truth is: I have feelings for you, and I have since the day I met you, when you were 17-years-old."

I barely looked up from the path we had reached and could scarcely breathe for fear of breaking the spell. My voice slid out in a whisper, "I feel the same way."

— now we wait —

"There have been so many times I've almost asked you out," Austin continued, as if afraid that if the words stopped they'd never start again. "Like the last time I visited you in Rochester. I came planning to ask you out, but didn't. I've prayed about it many times, but always thought God was saying, 'No.' The thing is, I no longer think He's saying 'no,' but I don't hear a 'yes' either. Not yet. And if I don't hear a 'yes,' then I think that means we should wait."

I nodded, drinking it all in.

"Tiffany, why do you even like me?" The question came so unexpectedly that I tipped my head back and laughed. "I know why I like *you*," he explained, "but what do you see in *me*? You've dated guys who were way better."

I shook my head. It's a gift and a curse, in a sense. The gift is that I can see the potential in people, sometimes even when they can't see it themselves. The curse is that sometimes the potential I see eclipses the reality of who they are in the present. I tried to tell him all the things I saw in him — his humor, objectivity, honesty, passion — but he just shook his head and said I didn't know him as well as I thought I did, that he wasn't the guy I thought he was. I refused to believe it, even though deep down I wondered if he was right: if the man I'd imagined wasn't the same Austin standing in front of me.

We talked then, like never before. About us, about the future, about the past; our barriers finally fallen. He said that if we started dating, it would be really serious, looking ahead to marriage. We'd known each other long enough to move in that direction from the start. So we talked about how marriage could work with my traveling and his job. We walked and talked for a couple hours, crickets slowly droning louder and louder, darkness falling faster and faster.

"I'm still seeing other girls too," he confided. "I have feelings for some of them too, so I'm not sure what that means." Neither did I. I blocked that statement almost entirely from my memory, as I had a habit of always wanting to forget the bad and only remember the good. "I don't want to lead you on, so unless we know this is definitely what we're supposed to do, we should wait."

It was strange how much closure I felt without coming to a conclusion. No matter what happened, at least now I knew I wasn't the only one who had felt these things or prayed these prayers. At least I would have no regrets one day, wondering what would have happened if I'd only been honest with him. At least I would never look back and wonder about the one that got away.

— who is austin? —

I was floating on bubbles. There's no other way to describe the giddy, teenage joy. I couldn't tell if it was love, or if it was the high of being chosen by the one you dreamed would choose you. Or, *almost* chosen, I suppose.

When I prayed about it, however, something didn't feel quite right. I couldn't figure it out. My intuition should line up with my excitement...*shouldn't it*? There was no way this could be wrong! Not after all these years.

Turns out I wasn't the only one who hadn't gotten any answers in my conversations with God. To be honest, things had gotten a little awkward between Austin and me. I tried to convince myself it was the whole, trying-to-move-to-more-than-friends drama, but there was something else going on.

We spent hours talking — drinking coffee and talking, hiking and talking, always talking. He opened up his heart to me in a way he never had before, but some of the things I saw were much different than who I thought he was. Just little things at first, but soon I began to have these haunting suspicions, like:

He wants to get married to make him happy. But marriage can never make someone happy; I can never make him happy. He has to be happy already.

Or, he doesn't really want to marry me; I'm just the good option right now. He's never fallen in love with me, his feelings are less than that. And I think that's why he's never dated me.

Or, *maybe all this time I've built him up in my mind and fallen in love with a man I've created, rather than with him. Maybe the man he is, isn't actually the man I think he is.*

And that hit the nail on the head. *Who was Austin?* Was he the Austin that Tiffany imagined — Tiffany who remembered only the good and not the bad? Austin himself had told me never to date a guy for his potential, because one could never tell if he'd reach it. But how I longed to call it out of him, to tell him all the things I saw in him and make them true by saying them! *Only life doesn't always work that way.*

Was I in love with Austin, the person, or with the idea of him? Normally I'd attribute these kinds of thoughts to my fears of relationships and say I just had commitment issues. *But this was different.* This was the one relationship I wasn't afraid of, the one relationship I craved with all my being. And it, too, seemed to be wrong.

When I shared these concerns with my aunt, she thought for a minute and then explained, "Some of these things you're telling me are big issues that speak to a person's character. I would take them seriously; don't just pass them by. We all sin and no one is perfect, but the fear of God is saying, 'I would rather cut off my arm than do anything that would displease God or separate me from Him.' That is the attitude you want to see in the man you marry."

She was right. Some of the issues he and I were talking through were pretty big issues. They weren't small things you could shake off and carry on without. Not things you could ignore, hoping they'd melt away like snow. *Because they wouldn't.*

I nodded, deep in thought, when my aunt rested her hand on my arm. "Tiffany, don't think God is too small to send you someone who's walking the same path as you."

Don't think God is too small. It was the last thing I wanted to hear, and yet the only thing that made sense. There were changes that needed to be made if we were ever to be together. It wasn't time for "us" just now, and perhaps there would never be an "us" — not with me and him, anyway.

But I *did* know this: *God had someone perfectly fitted for me.* It didn't mean my husband would be perfect, but our paths would meet and join. Maybe it would be with this man I cared for so deeply, but if it turned out that we weren't right for each other, then God had someone else for both of us. Neither of us would be missing out on anything. I just had to remember: *Don't think God is too small.*

— fireworks —

It was one of the final times we hung out that summer as slightly-more-than-friends. The humidity felt ready to burst over us, as I sat between what I'd dreamed my life would be, and the knowledge that it wasn't reality.

"Whoooooooaaaa!" A kid's chubby finger waved at Fourth of July fireworks high in the air. "It looks like Spiderman!"

I stifled a giggle and agreed, "Oh man, that one totally looks like Spiderman! That's so cool!"

Austin was quiet that night, perhaps thinking, perhaps just enjoying the moment under the stars. *Together.* My mind was clear, as though the rockets hurtling upward spoke to me, briefly disappearing before imploding into brilliant pieces, illuminating the air with glory. Their brokenness was also their beauty.

It was nice, *so nice* being there beside him. But I knew what I had to do.

Was I the only person in the world who came to Fourth of July celebrations with a man she cared for so deeply, all the while wondering if he'd be dating another girl tomorrow? Wondering who else would be in my place beside him next year?

And yet somehow, deep down, I wouldn't have it any other way. There was a fullness in the emptiness that was about to break over me; a peace in the uncertainty.

The display ended with a small finale, and thick, serene darkness descended like a blanket around us. I challenged myself to bring up what I knew I needed to say, but hesitated. *Maybe it can wait.* If I was lucky, he'd bring it up first; he'd be the one to say, "I don't think this is right," and I could simply agree. That would erase all further doubts from my mind.

Yes, it could wait. It would only spoil this one, last, perfect moment. Weaving through the crowds toward his car, I decided to leave *forever* for another day.

— the one who holds my heart —

Time passed too quickly, hurtling toward the honest conversation we inevitably had to have. I spent a couple weeks away at speaking engagements. During that time, we didn't talk *at all*. Neither of us initiated any conversation. That only made the decision more obvious. We were in love with the *idea* of each other. I was stuck on him just because he was the one that got away, the one I'd never quite been able to catch. Once I got home, I knew I couldn't put it off any longer.

Trees blurred together in my peripheral, Hillsong United's newest album providing the soundtrack, as I drove to meet him to talk about us. There in that moment, I felt as though time had frozen, despite the dotted highway lines which continued to flit past me in the blink of an eye. All I could see was that moment. *I knew what I had to do.*

For the briefest instant, grief swept over me and threatened to lock up my heart. I nearly choked on the words I was rehearsing, but then I remembered: *My Father delights in me.*

How different was this surrender than all the others. How different than when I knew I had to give up Eric, but wouldn't do it. What had changed in all these years? I shook my head to clear it, focusing on the road.

Maybe, on some off chance, this man would someday be mine and I would be his. But if not, everything within me knew that my Father would have something even better fitted for me. It was hard to imagine what that could look like, but I knew that He held the cattle on a thousand hills...*and He held my heart.*

That was it! That's what had changed in the last ten years! I finally believed, with everything inside me, that my Father held my heart, and He loved me. Really, truly loved me with a deep love I could never fully know. A love I still couldn't find the edges of. A love I'd spend my whole life discovering. Barreling toward that meeting, that decision, all I knew was His incredible delight in me, and even in its soft grief, my heart came alive.

Thirty minutes later, gelato dripped down Austin's cone and over his hands onto our outdoor seating. "That's why I asked for mine in a bowl," I teased.

"I know, I should've done that. Hold on, let me grab a napkin," he pulled open the door with his least-sticky fingers, emerging again with napkins fluttering in the wind.

I talked and talked for what seemed like ages. I hadn't seen him, or talked to him for that matter, in a few weeks, and there was so much to say. There was also so much I wanted to hear him tell me.

As we prepared to leave, I struck up the courage. "Wait, shouldn't we talk?"

"About what?" he asked.

"About us. We never came to a conclusion."

"Wait, we didn't talk about our decision?" he looked mystified. "I thought we decided it wasn't a good idea for us to date."

I breathed a sigh — was it relief or disappointment? — and gave a courageous laugh. "No, we never talked — not unless I'm totally losing my mind!"

"I thought for sure we did!" he shook his head. "Maybe I imagined it. I think that's what happened. I played out how the conversation would go in my head and thought we'd already had it. I'm so sorry."

"It's okay. I'm assuming we're both on the same page — that this isn't going to happen?"

"Yeah, that's what I was thinking."

"Okay. We're on the same page. We can go now."

"Are you sure?"

"Yes, totally." I felt lighter somehow, slipping naturally back into the friendship roles we'd always played.

Waving goodbye, the happiness slipped into nostalgia. I couldn't help wondering all the "what-if" questions, but of one thing I was certain: *I don't know what the future holds, but I know the One who holds my future. And, somehow, I trust Him.*

— Single and mostly sane —

Walking away from Austin was like finding everything I had been searching for. This boy-crazy girl had somehow found a semblance of sanity — and found it in her singleness, no less!

My mom said that as a child I would walk around the house, smiling up at the ceiling. When she asked what I was doing, I said, "I'm smiling up at God, because He's smiling at me." Over the years I lost that childlike trust that my heavenly Father delighted in me, but somehow during the last ten years since dating Eric, God had been restoring that faith to me: faith that He ruled the entire universe, yet still saw me. Faith that He was perfect, holy, and good. Faith that He had never once held out on me, because He'd given me Himself.

> *I don't know what the future holds, but I know the One who holds my future. And I trust Him.*

And I guess that was the purpose of everything I'd experienced: *To come closer to Him.* Not to get rid of my desire for marriage, but to surrender it. Not to change my emotions or circumstances, but to know Him more.

And isn't that the point of my story? The desire for marriage isn't wrong, but it's no longer a desperation. I don't have to get married to be okay. I don't have to find my Prince Charming to be happy. I'm already okay. I'm already happy. I've already found fullness of life in Christ. *And I've* found my purpose, which is this: to simply come closer to my heavenly Father each day that I live.

— a new story —

It was hard sometimes. Mostly during the blackness that comes before dawn, when your heart and memories awaken, but your mind isn't alert enough to crush the ache in your chest. Yet it was also beautiful. Like autumn leaves falling softly from trees. Letting go, disintegrating, so they can be made new.

Those were the words I began to hear, ever so slowly, ever so subtly, like whispers on the sunrise: *He makes all things new. Don't look back; look ahead. Ahead to where He is making all things new.*

Somewhere along the way, I'd begun to think Austin would be the man at the end of my love story; would, in fact, *be* my story. He had come to my rescue ten years ago, and many times in-between. We'd shared a myriad of moments, and I didn't want to start over with someone else. I didn't want to lose those memories tying us together.

But in the quietness of dawn, I felt God tugging at my soul. There was no obviously divine experience, no bold print in my Bible, just this quiet, peaceful assurance that steals your breath away when you notice it for the first time. One day, in the mundane motions of driving home, the thought came: *I think He's asking me to let go of Austin, so He can write a new story for me. To stop living in the old chapter, because He's writing something beautiful up ahead.*

So I'm letting go of all that has passed away, because the old is gone and He is already making all things new. My love story is only just beginning.

— the kind of love i've been waiting for —

I'm driving through the canyons of Utah, but I'm not lonely. Lavender, rose, and gold hues are splayed across the dunes. I've never seen terrain like this and had no idea how many colors adorn the desert, just as barrenness is cloaked with beauty, and loneliness with radiance.

And I know He's here.

He's been here, He is here, and He will always be here: right beside me.

I've been waiting my whole life for a love that will never leave, a love that will say I am enough even when I know I'm not. I've prayed and cried for a love to share adventures with, to write our stories together, to explore new ground and experience its beauty together. Always together.

I've craved someone to share life with. Every year that's gone by, I've felt desperation seep into my soul because of how much time has passed without that togetherness; how many adventures and stories I haven't gotten to share with my soul mate. This fear has crept in saying that he's missing out on so much life that we could have spent together, and wondering how many more stories I'll have to fill him in on, how many more adventures he'll miss that we could have experienced together. *I've wondered.*

But as I've spent this year driving all around the country with my boxes of books, touring all alone, I've found that I'm not lonely. In fact, *I'm full.* I'm full of lavender and rose and gold. I'm brimming with light and joy and hope. All this new territory I'm experiencing, all these incredible adventures — I'm sharing *every last one of them.* It's not just me on the journey. And it's *never* been just me on the journey.

Every story I've wanted to write with someone, every moment I've wanted to remember with someone, every tear and smile I've wanted to share and exclaim over and talk through with someone...*I've shared all of it.*

I've shared it with One who knows me better than I could ever know myself. With One who is patient and kind. One who dreams with me and for me. One who pursues me every day and who paints sunsets in my favorite colors when I am afraid. One who knows the depths of my heart. One who I can laugh with about my silly mistakes and One who will gladly listen to my ramblings... With the One who has never, not once, let me walk alone.

My Mentor.

My Companion.

My Best Friend.

My Lover.

I've shared *all* of it with Him.

It is worth every moment of waiting for my human prince because I've found a love that flows deeper, truer, and purer. I've made memories with the Lover of my soul more precious than any memory made with any guy I've dated. Just like the Utah desert, my lonely singleness has been clothed in beauty and become my thanksgiving, because I've found an intimacy beyond anything I've ever dreamed of. *I wouldn't trade this for the world.*

So I will wait as long as it takes for my human prince to come, because I know in my heart, that *this* — right here, right now — is the kind of love that people spend their whole lives waiting for.

HOW TO ENJOY SINGLENESS

Have you ever felt like life will start only once you get married? Because I've felt that way — like I was always waiting, waiting, waiting for my happily ever after. I didn't realize that my happily ever after had already begun! These are some ways that helped me enjoy life as a single person:

1) Find what makes you come alive. What talents, hobbies, or interests make you feel happy and fulfilled? Invest in those things! What better time than now? Someday when you're married with a family, you won't have as much time. Do you love music? Take lessons! Do you love traveling? Study abroad! Do you love politics? Find an internship in local government! *Now's the time!*

2) Serve others. There's no better way to get our eyes off of ourselves than to put them on other people. Get some friends together and make dinner at your local Ronald McDonald House, or join up with Habitat for Humanity. Run a 5K for a good cause, or volunteer at your church. Not only does service take our eyes off of our loneliness, but it also begins to connect us with the person we were created to be. It's more than just forgetting loneliness; it's becoming someone new, connecting with our heavenly purpose.

3) Develop deep friendships. Build meaningful relationships with both guys and girls. Friendships are incredibly important throughout life. Even after marriage, friends will fill places of your heart that your spouse cannot fill. Begin building those relationships now, and encouraging each other on your individual journeys.

4) Make a bucket list. If you're a goal-oriented person like me, this is a great way to feel less lonely. What things would be really fun to try? Sky diving? White water rafting? Reading 25 books a year? Make a list, and then check off each thing as you complete it!

5) Exercise. Seriously. It releases positive endorphins. As does chocolate.

6) Adopt an attitude of gratitude. Think of all the things you *have* rather than the things you *don't* have. The other day my friend Traci and I grabbed a latte before grocery shopping. As we stepped out of the car, I thought, *Out of all the people in the world, how is it that I'm in the tiny percentage of those who get to experience drinking a Starbucks latte while driving in a cute sporty car to go grocery shopping for a dinner party?* Thank God every day for the many blessings He's given you.

Focus on all the things you have, rather than on the things you don't have.

7) Ask, "Why do I crave a relationship so much?" It's absolutely natural, beautiful, and God-given to desire a marriage relationship. But sometimes it helps to ask ourselves, God, and those closest to us, "Why do you think I crave a relationship so much? What's the core desire beneath wanting a relationship? Is it a desire to be seen? To be loved? To no longer be alone?" And once you've found the core desire, ask this: "Right here and right now, how can God fill that desire?"

DISCUSSION QUESTIONS

Use these questions as part of a small group, with a mentor, or on your own. As you prayerfully reflect on these, feel free to journal your thoughts in the spaces below each question.

1) For a while, Austin was "the one that got away" in my life, always reappearing as an option. Do you have someone who got away? How do you know whether or not you should let that person go, so God can write a new chapter for you?

_____

_____

_____

_____

2) Do you ever imagine a guy to be something he's not? How can you see the reality of who someone is? How do you know if you're falling in love with him or with your idea of him?

_____

_____

_____

_____

3) Victory can already be ours, even before our circumstances have changed. What are some ways you've found victory in your life already? Even over the past few weeks, what are subtle changes you've seen God working into your heart?

_____

_____

_____

_____

4) Have you ever had one of those moments when it hits you in full color: "Oh! That's why thus-and-such happened! God did have a purpose after all!" What were some of those moments for you? How can those memories encourage you in every season of life, even singleness?

_____

_____

_____

_____

IF YOU'RE CURIOUS...

I like tying up stories in nice, neat packages. Life doesn't always work that way, but a lot has changed over the last year since I technically finished writing this book, which gives me the perspective to share a few stories of how God has been at work.

Eric: Though we don't keep in touch, I have forgiven Eric for the ways he treated me in our relationship. I also asked his forgiveness for the ways I treated him selfishly. It was the strangest experience to be asking forgiveness from someone who had hurt me so badly. He never realized all the ways he hurt me, but I realized that forgiveness is a choice that sets us free, and can be given without being requested. I'm not friends with him and don't expect to ever see him again, but he is forgiven. Last I heard, he was married and even a father; walking into the gifts and callings God has put on his life. I'm hopeful that he's changed a lot as he's grown older, and it sounds like God is doing great things in and through him, which brings joy to my heart.

Karl: We're what you'd call social media friends. Seeing as he's on the other side of the world, I haven't seen him since my time in Australia. However, I love keeping up with him via social media, watching his church is grow (yup, he's a missionary/pastor now!), seeing pictures of his beautiful wife and son, and celebrating from afar what God is doing with the dreams in his heart.

Travis: When I see Travis (and his new girlfriend who is seriously PERFECT for him!!), things aren't awkward. He's such a great guy that there are no hard feelings. I am so pumped for him with the new career path he's chosen and with the girl in his life who loves him beyond words, in a way I never could have!

Austin: I just saw him a couple days ago, and in fact asked him if he wanted to read this book before I published it. He asked, "Are you going to make me sound good?" and when I said yes, he grinned, "Then of course publish it! It'll be the nicest thing anyone has ever said about me!" I'm glad we still get to share our stories together, that our friendship is strong enough that nothing seems to be able to shake it. He also began dating this amazing girl a few months ago, and I really like her! She's down to earth, real, and fun to hang out with. And, as a matter of fact, they are planning to double date with me and this guy I've begun dating...

Yup, you heard me right. (Insert smiley face here.) I'll be 28 in a matter of weeks. No ring on my finger. Still traveling and speaking for my job. Watching God work in amazing ways, so beyond excited for what the future holds. And out of the blue, just a couple months ago, this guy walked into my life. The strangest thing is that I have no fear or hesitation about being with him. He's seriously incredible...I could go on for pages and chapters, but that's for another book, another story. Who knows what will come of our relationship? But of this I am sure: I don't know what my future holds, but I know the One who holds my future.

And I trust Him.

ABOUT THE AUTHOR

Tiffany Dawn is a 28-year-old dreamer, adventurer, songwriter, and author of <u>The Insatiable Quest for Beauty</u> and <u>Boycrazy</u>. She speaks in high schools, colleges, churches, and treatment centers across the United States for audiences of all ages and both genders, but her truest passion is sharing her story with teen and college-age girls. With her master's degree in music therapy, Tiffany's dream is to open a home for girls struggling with eating disorders. She has a not-so-secret love affair with raspberry chai, long walks, and everything CIA. When she's not escaping winter through cross-country tours (to the warm states), Tiffany resides in beautiful upstate New York.

Visit www.tiffanydawn.net to learn more.

CHECK OUT TIFFANY'S FIRST BOOK AND MUSIC ALBUM: